outreach
MINISTRY
in the 21st century

the encyclopedia of practical ideas

Reach the world.
Explore the Bible.
Serve others.

Share Jesus.

Group

Loveland, Colorado
www.group.com

Group resources actually work!

This Group resource helps you focus on **"The 1 Thing™"**—a life-changing relationship with Jesus Christ. "The 1 Thing" incorporates our **R.E.A.L.** approach to ministry. It reinforces a growing friendship with Jesus, encourages long-term learning, and results in life transformation, because it's:

Relational
Learner-to-learner interaction enhances learning and builds Christian friendships.

Experiential
What learners experience through discussion and action sticks with them up to 9 times longer than what they simply hear or read.

Applicable
The aim of Christian education is to equip learners to be both hearers and doers of God's Word.

Learner-based
Learners understand and retain more when the learning process takes into consideration how they learn best.

Credits
Editor: Carl Simmons
Quality Control Editor: Dave Thornton
Chief Creative Officer: Joani Schultz
Copy Editor: Ann Jahns
Cover Art Directors/Designers: Jean Bruns and Kevin Mullins
Interior Art Directors: Nancy Serbus and Jeff Storm
Print Production Artist: Nancy Serbus
Illustrator: Alan Flinn
Production Manager: DeAnne Lear

Unless otherwise indicated, all Scripture quotations are taken from the *Holy Bible*, New Living Translation, copyright © 1996, 2004. Used by permission of Tyndale House Publishers, Inc., Wheaton, Illinois 60189. All rights reserved.

Library of Congress Cataloging-in-Publication Data

Outreach ministry in the 21st century : the encyclopedia of practical ideas.
    p. cm.
  ISBN-13: 978-0-7644-3437-2 (pbk. : alk. paper)
 1. Evangelistic work--Handbooks, manuals, etc. 2. Church work--Handbooks, manuals, etc. I. Group Publishing.
  BV3790.O86 2007
  269'.2--dc22

                            2006033427

10 9 8 7 6 5 4 3 2 1   16 15 14 13 12 11 10 09 08 07
Printed in the United States of America

TABLE OF CONTENTS

Section 5: 20 Movie Nights

Section 7: Caring for the Long Haul: Ideas for Long-Term Service..................... 170

9 Ways to Serve Your Children and Youth 172

16 Ways to Reach Out to Adults in Need 180

Contributors

Thanks to the following men and women—pastors, writers, and leaders of outreach ministries—for providing the dozens of ideas in this volume.

Pamela Enderby

Dr. Dave Gallagher

Cheri R. Gillard

Linda Holloway

Jan Kershner

Jeanette Gardner Littleton

Mark Littleton

Keith Madsen

A. Koshy Muthalaly

Kristi Rector

Larry Shallenberger

David Trujillo

Kelli Trujillo

Amber Van Schooneveld

Michael Van Schooneveld

Heather Werle

Paul Woods

INTRODUCTION

Introduction

Welcome to *Outreach Ministry in the 21st Century: The Encyclopedia of Practical Ideas!*

Most Christians understand the importance of sharing their faith with the world around them. Knowing how and where to take those first steps in sharing, however, is often tough. This book is here to make those steps easier for you—and enjoyable as well, as your church learns how to reach out to friends, neighbors, co-workers, community members, and others in ways that are both surprisingly easy and surprisingly effective.

You'll find dozens upon dozens of practical ideas here to use. Best of all, you can begin putting many of them into practice as soon as you're ready to start! These ideas are creative, practical, and hands-on. Whether you want to put together an activity to deepen relationships, discuss the Christian themes in a secular movie, dive in to a service project for the disadvantaged in your community, or commit to a more long-term relationship with those who really need to know the love of Jesus, this book can help.

Because this book is a collection of practical ideas, we've worked hard to put it together in a practical way. You can read it cover to cover, or you can pick and choose the ideas you need *right now*. You might want to start in the Table of Contents, locate the kind of outreach ministry you'd like to get involved in, and scan the tips and ideas from there.

TO COPY

You may want to put copies of many of these pages in the hands of those working alongside you. Therefore, please note that several pages throughout this book have been noted as "OK to copy." (Look for the logo shown in the margin.)

We pray that both you and those you serve will reap eternal benefits from the ideas in this book. May God bless and use you and your ministry.

—Carl Simmons, Editor

SECTION 1

Making Your Church Visible

Here

YOU'VE picked up this book because you're here to live like Jesus. And you already know that a big part of that is getting out into your community and serving the needs you see around you. But for many churches—especially younger ones—just getting on your community's radar so you're in a position to *discover* those needs can be a big challenge.

The ideas in this opening section are here to get you started down that road. They'll give you some practical ways to say, "Hi, we're your neighborhood church, and we're here to help." And they're ideas your church will enjoy doing, so next time you hit the streets it'll be that much more enjoyable and effective.

Whether you hold events in your church building or set up a booth at a local event, these ideas will help your church to stick your foot in the door of your community—in ways that are caring, fun, and illuminating for both your church and your community.

8 Ideas to Get Your Church Noticed

Idea 1   Sticker Shock—of a *Good* Kind

Sticker shock at the gasoline pump is a subject on nearly everyone's mind these days. Ease a little bit of the burden in your own community by lowering the price of gas at a chosen gas station for a few hours one Saturday. You'll see lines at the pump, but drivers will all have smiles on their faces for a change!

Here's how it would work: Your church would pledge and collect a specific amount of money. Before your event, go to your congregation to raise the necessary funds. Explain that your church would like to offer a benefit to the community by helping people lower their gasoline prices at the pump. That money would be used to allow customers at a specific gas station in your town to pay less at the pump for a few hours on a given day. For example, if the regular price of gas is $3.00, your church could enable customers to buy the same gas at $2.75 from 11 a.m. to 1 p.m. on a specified Saturday.

Next, find a local gas station at a prominent intersection. Ask the owner if your church could take two hours on a Saturday to offer gasoline at prices lower than the regular cost. Explain that your church will make up the difference. Say that your church simply wants to do something helpful for the community. (It wouldn't hurt to point out that the event will probably garner the gas station lots of free publicity!)

Ask the owner approximately how much gas the station sells during the specified two hours on any given Saturday. This will give you an idea of how much money your church needs to raise.

This event will likely result in long lines at the pump. For once, that's a good thing! So don't be conservative in your fundraising estimations. The more money you collect before the event, the more you can give away!

Before the big day, make lots of signs that tell the "new" price of gas and the hours it will be offered. Make sure your church's name is clearly displayed.

If you want to go the extra mile, have church volunteers offer drivers soft drinks as they wait their turn at the pump. Kids from your youth group could be available to wash windows as an added service. And when anyone asks why your church is sponsoring such an event, just say that you want to help people and spread the love of God around town!

Idea 2   Car Carriers

Here's an idea that not only helps you reach out to the community but gets your church plenty of notice, too!

Choose a local store that gets plenty of foot traffic. Your neighborhood Wal-Mart, grocery store, or home improvement center are all good choices. Speak with the store's manager, and explain that members of your church would like to spend a few hours on an upcoming Saturday to help patrons get their carts to their cars and unload their purchases. Together, decide which hours of the day would be most beneficial to shoppers. Emphasize that no strings are attached!

On your chosen Saturday, position volunteers near exits of the store. As people come out, offer to help them get their carts to their cars and load their purchases in the vehicles. Elderly shoppers and moms with small children might be most appreciative.

Before the event, have T-shirts printed with the name and address of your church. You might also want to print simple fliers to hand out that give your church's name, address, telephone number, Web address, service times, and a simple welcoming invitation. If you do this, offer a flier to each person, but don't force the information on anyone. Your goal here is to simply offer cheerful help in a way that allows your love of Jesus to shine in your actions.

If children from your church are involved in this project, make sure an adult accompanies each child or group of children as they move off into the parking lot. Never let a child offer assistance alone.

Idea 3　Support Your Local Team

Odds are that many in your community are involved (or are the parent of a child who's involved) with a sports event or program in your area—whether it's a youth program, a high school team, or an adult sports league. So show your support and become a sponsor. Here are just a few ideas:

- Get a sponsor sign put up on the fence at a baseball or football game (or a banner, for an indoor sport).
- Sponsor a local Little League team, and put your church's name on T-shirts.
- Sponsor a local softball or bowling team (or start one!).
- Sponsor a car at a local speedway. (C'mon, can't you just see your church's name on the side?)
- Become a partial sponsor of a community event.
- Help pay for programs at high school sports events (and get your name in the program).

Don't just limit your church's participation to financial sponsorship, though—find ways to participate at the events you help sponsor. Your church can distribute programs, serve free beverages (maybe hot chocolate at cold football games) or snacks, or assist in the running of the event. Or maybe you can supply fruits or drinks for both teams at halftime or at the end of the event. Let them know you're there for them—both on and off the field.

Idea 4　NASCAR Race Day

If you want to do something different to catch the attention of people in your community, *here's* an event to try!

Contrary to common perceptions, NASCAR fans come from all levels of society—and they will be pleasantly surprised to have you tailor an event to their interests.

A month or more in advance, check the NASCAR Nextel Cup Series schedule (www.nascar.com/races), and determine a race that you'd like to show on a big screen for race fans in your community. Be sure you have a good video projector, screen, sound system, and TV hookup for the right channel. (An outdoor showing would be even more fun, but daylight may make it impossible to get a good image from the projector.)

If you can possibly use an area of your church, your community may well be intrigued that a church would promote such an event on church grounds. If you need to use a facility other than your church, be sure to make it clear that your church is sponsoring the entire event. Spread the word by handing out fliers at a local racetrack. You could also put up posters in local hangouts and around town.

Plan and advertise free refreshments. You might want to make it clear in all advertising that you'll allow no alcoholic beverages or drunkenness. You'll probably also want to decide in advance what your policy on smoking will be.

Even if attendance at your event isn't overwhelming, people in your community will begin to catch the idea that your church is a *little* different!

Idea 5   Preen a Park

Commit to caring for a particular park in your area. Survey the park and see what you could do to improve its looks or usability. Some ideas might be to use a lawn edger along the sidewalks, fertilize or reseed areas of sparse grass, add additional or better cushioning material under swings, paint or varnish playground equipment, or plant flowers or other attractive vegetation.

Develop a plan for what you realistically can and are willing to do. Then set up an appointment and talk to the parks department of your city government. Lay out your plan, and make it clear that your commitment does not reflect negatively on their care of the park, but that you simply want to make that park especially nice for the community. You might want to suggest a one-year trial basis, during which both your church and the community can evaluate the project.

Once you have permission, keep your commitment. If anything, go above and beyond what you've agreed to do. Report to the city any repair needs, and do them yourselves only if they give you specific permission. After things are going well, ask the city if you could place a small sign at the entrance to the park that says, "This park lovingly cared for by [your church]."

Once things are looking especially nice, ask your local newspaper to do an article to highlight what you're doing. You might even write the article yourself and send it along with photos. If you do so, use a reporter's viewpoint rather than writing a fluff piece—your piece will have more credibility with readers if you use this perspective.

Preening a park can create a positive buzz for your church in the community. And as your people work, they may even have opportunities to talk with park users about your church and our Lord.

Idea 6   Halloween Handouts

On Halloween evening, your church members of all ages can accomplish the unexpected as you go out trick-or-treating—by giving treats *to* your neighbors instead.

Within a mile radius of your church, go house to house, offering candies, snacks, or candles donned with a ribbon and a note. On your note, print a Scripture verse or perhaps a simple message like "Jesus is the light of the world," and include your church's contact information and Web site address if you have one.

You'll discover that giving treats softens hearts. If you ask your neighbors if they have any needs you can pray for, many will respond positively. Use sensitivity as you ask and in deciding *when* to ask. But if you do ask, take time to jot down prayer requests, coupled with their names, addresses, and, if they're willing to share, phone numbers. Ask permission to share these requests with others if you plan on doing so, and also be sure to ask if you can contact them for updates.

Give any prayer requests you receive to your outreach coordinator when all your Halloween heralds reconvene at the church for a post-Halloween Handout party. Share prayer requests with your congregation's prayer team. Their follow-up prayers, notes of encouragement, and phone calls give your church another friendly opportunity to become visible—and to make the love of Jesus real to others.

Idea 7   Adopt a Block

Almost every community has areas where residents have trouble taking care of their homes and lawns. Many homeowners are discouraged by poverty or disabilities. Your church can make a difference in their lives, and by doing so you can make your church more visible to the neighborhood around or near you.

Select a block of homes in your community, and work with your city government to adopt that block. Be sure you have a feasible plan to present to the city, and be sure you have enough volunteers to accomplish what you're proposing. Some things you might include in the plan are picking up trash, raking leaves, mowing or grooming lawns, trimming shrubs and trees, planting new grass, painting homes, or rebuilding porches. The only limit is what you can agree on with the city and with homeowners. Also, make sure you have an understanding with the city about how much you can share about your faith as you work.

After getting permission to proceed, develop a flier that describes what you want to do, and talk to each homeowner on the block. If homes are rented, you'll need to talk to both the landlord and the tenant. Ask residents what they'd like you to do for them, within the scope of your plan—then follow through.

When things are going well, ask your city government if you can put up a sign similar to the "adopt a highway" signs you see along highways. Give each person on the block a card or a folder about your church, and take every opportunity to engage residents in conversation and build relationships with them. Soon people around your community will be asking, "When are you coming to *my* block?"

Idea 8   Car Show

Even those who aren't car enthusiasts are often curious to check out a classic or antique car. So invite those who *are* car enthusiasts to bring classic cars to display in your community. As your church interacts with those with similar interests, relationships can develop that eventually draw people toward faith in Christ.

Offer prizes to car owners and free food and drink to onlookers. If possible, avoid charging anything for people to come and see the cars. If you charge an entrance fee, make sure that any proceeds go toward the prizes or to some other good cause.

You'll need to begin planning this event as much as six months in advance. Before setting a date for your car show, you'll want to check event schedules around the area, particularly those related to classic-car enthusiasts. Plan your event when the weather is most likely to be nicest and when there are the fewest conflicting events in the area.

Begin advertising the event several months in advance. Make it clear what kinds of cars qualify for your show and where registration forms can be obtained. You'll want to be sure any rules you have regarding what can be done on church grounds are clear to car owners. For example, if you want to prohibit alcoholic beverages, smoking, or loud music, you'll want to have that written out and agreed to by all registrants.

Recruit lots of volunteers to help at the event, and have them wear "event staff" shirts or badges. Encourage them to interact with car owners and onlookers alike. Be careful not to be too pushy about faith-sharing, but be ready to explain why you're holding this event and to answer people's questions about your church and faith.

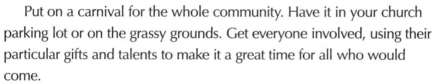

10 Ideas for Community Events

Idea 1   Community Carnival

Kids of all ages love carnivals. From the ring toss to the cakewalk, the dunking machine to the pony rides, there's something for everyone!

Put on a carnival for the whole community. Have it in your church parking lot or on the grassy grounds. Get everyone involved, using their particular gifts and talents to make it a great time for all who would come.

Snacks like bags of popcorn, candy, huge hot pretzels, cotton candy, and snow cones are always welcomed treats. Machines can be rented to make carnival treats, or you can create and use your own setup.

Rented blow-up bouncers and amusement rides are always a hit, as well as miniature or Frisbee golf courses, squirt-gun tag games, bowling, a water-balloon toss, a giant bubble maker, and the age-and-weight-guessing game.

Roaming entertainers will add to the fun. Recruit closet magicians or clowns from your congregation (*real* clowns, that is!), or hire some to come and join the fun. Musicians will be sure to please, whether they provide concerts or provide wandering entertainment. Strolling singers can add a laugh by singing requests or changing lyrics on the spot to fit a situation.

Let the day culminate with an outdoor evening performance under the stars by a musical group, a comedy presentation, or perhaps a fireworks display. (Be sure to check your city ordinances for any activities you plan.)

Whatever you decide, make sure the whole community knows they are welcome. Advertise to the public. Obtain local merchants' involvement, if possible. Use the opportunity to introduce those who live around you to be a part of what's happening at your church—and enjoy some good, old-fashioned fun!

Idea 2 Town Festival

Most large communities hold annual or even seasonal town festivals. Use the day as an opportunity for your church to get to know and serve others in your town. Make arrangements with festival coordinators (at least a few weeks in advance) to set up a table or booth for that day—they're often free to civic groups. Then, decide on how you want to serve those who stop by to say hello (or walk around and meet them, if you like).

Be as elaborate or as simple in your planning as you like. Have some inexpensive but meaningful giveaways available, such as baked goods and coffee, or upgrade your food offerings to a lunch of sodas and sub sandwiches. (One church that did this also took up a collection for the Girl Scouts selling similar foods at a booth nearby, to make up for "stolen business.")

Give away balloons or small gifts to kids who are walking around, and have lots of extra balloons available for when kids inevitably lose them. Better yet, hire a clown to give out the balloons, and take Polaroids of the kids posing with him or her. This would also free up your volunteers to spend more time talking to visitors.

Or take it to the next level, and offer concerts, plays, or puppet shows as part of your church's contribution to the day. Whatever you do, make a point of enjoying this time among the rest of your community. Don't only be generous with your resources but also with your time and attention. Not only will your festival time be a good body-building exercise, but it will also be an opportunity to show the community a different kind of "(church) family fun."

Idea 3 Sharing the Arts

Chances are there are many artistic and creative people in your church. They may paint in oils or watercolors, be gifted in photography, or do crafts such as pottery or embroidery. Provide an opportunity for your gifted artists to display their talents during an all-day arts festival.

Invite everyone in your church and community to come see the wonderful variety of artistic expression in your church. Encourage each artist to bring samples of his or her work—and if it's possible, have him or her work on new projects during the event.

Some artists may also want to provide supplies and give demonstrations of their crafts so that visitors can try their hand at it as well. For example, painters may set up extra easels with canvasses or paper, or potters may provide clay for hand-building. You may also want to have the artists offer classes in the future to those interested in learning how to do each kind of art.

You may also consider having live music at your event. Have music playing in the background either way, for atmosphere—and at a level where people can still converse easily.

Have fun creating as well as supporting those who create. Also have fun getting to know the people in your church and your community better.

Idea 4   MLK Day Celebration

In many communities, Martin Luther King Day is a holiday without a celebration, especially in communities that are not African-American. Many have the day off, but because it's in the middle of winter, they don't have anything special planned. Take advantage of the real significance of this holiday to make a statement about human community and justice—and at the same time add some multicultural sensitivity to your church.

Be aggressive: Invite the mayor or another high official of your city. Make sure you have a good speaker and good music. Try to get a minister to speak from an African-American perspective. The speaker is especially important, as civic-sponsored celebrations often fail to acknowledge the role of Dr. King's faith in his quest for justice and racial equality. It is particularly important to start early recruiting these participants, as African-American preachers and singers are often busy at this time of the year.

Make sure that your own pastor has a prominent role in the service so that people who are looking for a church with multicultural sensitivity will become acquainted with him or her and know where he or she stands.

Idea 5　On This Day in (Local) History...

Every community has its share of unsung (or no-longer-sung) heroes who helped shape what that community is today. Find one such person who's under-recognized in the history of your city or region, and design a day to honor him or her. Use the day to instill some community pride as well as to get to know and have fun with others in your community.

Get suggestions from your local historical society or from reading a local history. Identify what about this person is really unique and deserving of recognition, then take that person's special qualities or ideas and build your event around it.

Set up booths, displays, and games in your community center, park, or church. Include games that people played at the time of your historical figure or craft booths to display and create crafts of the period. Contact a community drama group, or have your church's drama team dress up in period costumes and do an interactive drama based on your special person's life. (Do this on the church lawn or parking lot, where it can be seen by passers-by!)

Notify local schools or kids' groups ahead of time, and encourage them to bring classes or groups as a field trip. Invite a local history expert to speak; make sure he or she is a good speaker who can relate to both children and adults. Let him or her speak for only about 20 minutes tops, though, as you want to keep this event an interactive experience.

Idea 6　Be True to Your School

With many school budgets suffering, school grounds are in bad shape. Connect with a local school and agree to recruit volunteers to come and clean up the school grounds in August before school starts. You will need someone to be in charge of recruiting helpers, someone to be in charge of the work site itself, and someone to be in charge of a meal or refreshment time.

Recruits should come from the whole community, not just from your church. This is your chance not only to show your church's concern for the children and youth of the community but also to connect with their parents—many of whom may be looking for a church that is involved in this way. Recruit through your local media but also through the friendship connections of parents and children in your church.

The work site leader should work with the principal and custodian(s) of the school to determine which projects can best be done by volunteers. Divide up projects and areas of the grounds into sections, and assign teams of volunteers to each section, with one person assigned as the section leader. Make sure that people from your church team up with other community people and hence get to know them.

Tasks that often need to be done include bush trimming, weed pulling, litter collecting, and spreading of bark dust. Check with local landscapers to see if one would donate bark dust or other needed material for the cause. Assign volunteers to bring needed tools, like weed whips, hedge trimmers, hand tools for pulling weeds, and plastic lawn debris bags. Volunteers should be asked to bring their own work gloves and water bottles.

After the cleanup, invite people to your church for a meal or time of refreshments. Make sure that your pastor is there, and introduce him or her to the other workers.

Idea 7　Serve the Servants

Not every service idea has to originate with your church or compete with "other things going on in town." Why not have the best of both worlds and use your time to show appreciation and support for others already serving or supporting those in your community?

Identify an all-day charity event that will be held in your community in the next month or so. Make arrangements with the organizers to set up a booth either at the event or—if it's a charity walk—along the route that participants are traveling through your town. Set up a table or a tent, and put out a banner or poster to invite participants to come take a break. (A tent will help protect participants from the elements, so those you're serving get even more needed relief—and you can last longer, too!)

Have a selection of fresh fruits, healthy snacks, and water bottles available to support and refresh those participating in the event or attending in support. Find out in advance how many are expected to attend so you have enough supplies on hand. Local stores are also often willing to contribute food and supplies for a good cause. Once you've established what you'd like to give away, approach store managers about partnering with you.

Some charity events go all night, too, so think about the degree of commitment you want to make, then stick to it.

Be sure to take time to speak with those who visit, and encourage them in the good work they're doing or taking the time to support. It will give everyone an extra spiritual and emotional boost, even as you're addressing their physical needs.

Idea 8   Guess Who's Coming to Dinner?

Have a day where you invite law enforcement officers as your guests at a dinner, and use the day to not only express some long-overdue respect but to build relationships with the officers and their families.

Invite a speaker who has some expertise in the area of law enforcement and who can help others appreciate all the things the officers do. You may also want to invite those you know who have especially benefited from law enforcement in the last year—people who have had property recovered, people who have had officers stop and help when they were stranded, or people who have been victims of crime where the criminals were caught and convicted—so they can share their appreciation. Invite people from a variety of cultures, if possible. Make sure, however, that everyone you invite is there with the intention of encouraging your guests of honor and is truly grateful for their service.

Invite your local newspaper to cover the event, if you like. Point out how important it is to the community to honor law enforcement, and make sure they're aware of the qualifications of your speaker and guests and their accomplishments in the community.

Idea 9   School's-Out Block Party

Give the kids near your church area a special day at the end of the school year. Begin by prayerfully considering which block of homes near your church you'll hold the event at and the day and time you'll set. Then, spread the news!

On your party day—and with permission from your local officials—block off the street. Oftentimes, the town will provide road construction barriers for you. Then stake a banner, saying, "Hurray! School Is Out!…Sponsored by [your church]."

Serve ice-cold lemonade, and crank up the popcorn and snow cone machines if you have them. Kids attract kids, so involve your church's youth in putting on skits and puppet shows. Plan more games and activities than you think you need, in case kids run through them quickly. Games that allow for group winners instead of individual winners are more likely to eliminate tears and frustration over losing.

Finally, finish off your block party with Polaroid snapshots of each guest to hand out to them as they leave so they have a memento of the party fun. Include your church's address label on the back of each picture.

And when summer ends, reach out to the same bunch of kids—only this time, call it a "Back-to-School Party"!

Idea 10   Community (Pre-)Christmas Party

Christmastime is, for many, less a time for remembering the birth of Jesus and more a time to dwell on the many headaches and hassles of the holiday season. Give your community a chance to unwind from their holiday stress—and remind them of the *real* meaning of Christmas—by throwing a Pre-Christmas Party!

Plan a date in early December, when the shopping season is near its peak but before all the other Christmas parties get started. Set up your church—or a building that's big enough to hold a crowd and near enough to local shops to be visible—for your party. Take your party into the evening if you like, but be sure to be open during the day so Christmas shoppers can just wander in and relax for a spell.

It probably goes without saying to provide lots of good food and refreshments, but also be sure to provide entertainment and services. You'll likely get a lot of parents with kids, so provide games and puppet shows. Have some live music, and be sure to include some Christmas carols. Also, offer free gift-wrapping services for anyone who brings in gifts. You could even offer massages for tired shoppers badly in need of de-stressing.

And of course, have a live Nativity in front of your party location. Remind people what this holiday is *really* about.

8 Opportunities for Special Events in Your Church

Idea 1   Striking the Right Chord

Accent the *natural* musical talent of your church, and put on a potpourri of music. Whether you *measure* your available talent by professional musicians or those who just love to use their musical gifts for enjoyment, you can pull together an extraordinary evening of entertainment that's sure to be a *major* hit that can't be *beat* in your community.

Recruit musical acts and organize the format of your performance. Be as focused or eclectic as you want. Perhaps you will want to have a concert of all classical music, or maybe your church's *forte* will be more along the lines of pop and rock music, or jazz and blues. Determine if you will have secular or Christian music, or both.

Recruiting a known performer or group for the final act may be the *key* to add both anticipation and draw. Local churches often have connections to Christian rock bands or other performing ensembles.

Let the whole community know of your concert. Local radio stations are a good source to help *pitch* your idea and promote your event. Don't *fret*. They will often make announcements free of charge.

During the course of the evening, encourage band members to take a break and move around the audience, just getting to know people and befriending them. This is not the time to share the gospel or even talk about church or the Bible, just to build relationships.

Your concert can be a great *overture* to a friend or an easy way to bring outsiders into the church without asking any thing of them but to come and have a *fine* time!

Idea 2   Auction Block

Arrange an auction (silent and/or live) of services, artwork, products, baked goods, or any other saleable and quality items your church can offer. Use the opportunity to provide services to and develop relationships with those outside your church.

Brainstorm for creative, unique ideas and items to auction off. Consider the extravagant. For example, offer an evening of exquisite dining and entertainment by having a talented cook prepare a gourmet dinner for four at the buyer's own home. Make it extra-special by including a live musician to provide background music.

Include the practical. Recruit a CPA to donate an hour or two of accounting or tax assistance—or recruit other professionals to provide services unique to their vocation. Other easier-to-find but useful ideas include babysitting hours, housecleaning, yard/car care, painting (house painting or decorative wall murals), portraits (drawn, painted, or photographed), and pet care.

For physical health and luxury, an hour massage from a certified massage therapist is a choice idea. Or consider auctioning off gym time or a facial and makeover with a beauty consultant.

If you do a live auction, have the persons offering the services stand up front while the auctioneer calls for and accepts bids.

Form a committee to organize the event and recruit donations. Be careful to avoid auctioning items that would be better off going to the thrift store—or worse yet, the dumpster. Encourage the whole church to become involved in the event. Kids and adults—entire families—can participate. Determine the recipient of the proceeds—such as a local family who lost their home, a group of orphans, or a mission—and use that cause to inspire and motivate participation.

Area restaurants will often donate gift certificates. Persons with their own business, such as photographers or seamstresses, can offer popular packages. Any person who is in retail or sales might have resources within his or her business to obtain quality items that others will value and desire. These kinds of items work well in both live and silent auctions. If you choose to put these in a silent auction, be sure to allow enough time for all the items to be reviewed and for bids to be collected, as well as communicate a reasonable and precise ending time.

Idea 3   Computer Game Tournament

Many young people and even adults are passionate about computer games. Why not bring a bunch of computers to your church and have a tournament? The entry fee can be a couple of cans of food for the local food bank, and you can offer a plaque or trophy for the winner.

Make sure you choose games that are not multilevel and that can be completed in a reasonable period of time. Ask the teenagers and young adults of your church for suggestions of games that do not last a long time. Some games can be judged on best time, others on most points. On games that are won according to most points, you may want to stipulate that whoever gets the most points within a designated period of time wins, in order to keep things from going on too long.

Appoint a couple of monitors to keep track of scores and to make sure rules are followed. Have a time at the end where trophies are presented and where people can have refreshments and hang out afterward.

Idea 4   *Which* Creation?

As the creationism vs. evolution debate rages on, even many Christians are left confused about what to believe. Your church can learn to respond intelligently to the questions that are raised and invite the community to join in the debate in a civil and informed manner.

Do some research online, and ask others you know in the ministry to refer you to a top-notch creation scientist. Schedule an evening when the creation scientist can make an appearance. Advertise the event on campuses, at coffeehouses, in bookstores, and in places where people gather. Be sure to extend the invitation to anyone you know who would like to ask questions of the scientist.

If you want to invite an evolution scientist to argue the other side, do so. Use it as an opportunity to love him or her as Jesus would. When non-Christians discover that the Bible (and Christians) can intelligently respond to questions they may have, they may be more open to exploring the rest of God's claims in his Word as well.

Idea 5   Money Matters

Many people today are worried about retirement, if they're not already struggling with financial matters. Even those people who know how to put together a budget—and a surprising number of people don't—would like to get a better handle on how to stretch their dollars these days.

Plan an event to teach members of your community how to handle their money, and get the word out! Make your target audience as specific or broad as you choose (and depending on your selection of presenters). This event would be very beneficial for single men and women who are just starting out, for teens, and for anyone who would like to learn more about money.

Invite experts who work in the financial world, from within your church and without, to teach classes on topics such as saving money, getting out of debt, learning to tithe, learning about stocks and bonds, and planning for large purchases. (Be clear about your expectations in presenting information from a Christian perspective, especially if you bring in outside speakers.)

There are also prepackaged financial course kits available that explore these issues from a Christian perspective. Crown Financial Ministries (www.crown.org) and Willow Creek's Good $ense Ministry (www.goodsenseministry.org) are two such ministries that provide solid financial curricula.

Idea 6   Super Soup and Pie

People love to eat. And who doesn't like homemade baked pie or free baked goods? Let those who wouldn't normally come through your doors experience a nonthreatening event where nothing is asked of them but to sit down with you and enjoy some good food and fun.

Organize a Super Soup and Pie Supper, and invite everyone to come and enjoy a warm welcome from your church, in the form of a hot bowl of soup and a fresh-baked piece of pie. Add some extra fun and anticipation to your event by giving out door prizes at regular intervals.

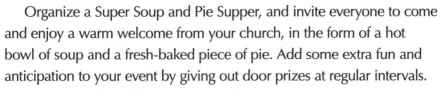

Cooks within your church family can prepare large pots of soup or stew—give a variety of choices, if possible. Fresh-baked pies, made and donated by church members, will round out the simple supper nicely and keep the burden from falling on any one person.

Also collect other baked goods—such as cakes, muffins, cinnamon rolls, or additional pies—to give as door prizes. Have diners put their names in a hat, and draw as frequently or infrequently as you're able to reward your visitors.

You might ask for a nominal fee of a couple of dollars from each person, or offer the meal for free if your church has the resources to cover the cost. Be sure to advertise well, spreading the word through fliers, posters, radio announcements, ticket distribution, and/or word of mouth. Encourage everyone to purchase tickets and give them away to the people they know. Challenge every member of your church to invite at least one or two neighbors to come and enjoy a hot bowl of soup, some delicious pie, and a chance to meet some new friends.

Idea 7   **Parenting Seminar**

Even the best parents need some more wisdom from time to time (or reassurance that they really *are* on the right track!). Show that your church cares about families by hosting a parenting seminar for your community.

Invite an outside speaker (or two or three especially gifted parents in your own congregation) to give talks on topics relevant to your attendees. Include a panel of parents for an open-question session. Among the topics you can discuss:

- how to set boundaries with teenagers
- the challenges of single parenting

RECOMMENDED RESOURCE:

One great small-group series that will help you explore parenting ideas in more depth, and from a biblical perspective, is the HomeBuilders Parenting Series® (Group).

- building character in your children
- maintaining a healthy marriage for the sake of healthy children
- understanding and developing your children's faith
- insights into how your child's (or teen's) brain really works
- parenting with love and logic

Provide a pleasant, warm atmosphere. Include a wide selection of refreshments. Have students and adult volunteers greet parents and show them to their seats. Use this opportunity to show your community what a church family looks like, too.

Don't stop at your seminar, though. Provide opportunities for both your attendees and you to follow up on what they've learned. Contact participants to attend your church or other related events there, or offer short-term small groups on the subject you've covered.

Idea 8   Wedding Workshop

One of the most opportune moments to establish meaningful contact with the young adults in your community is during engagement time. Try something a little different—offer an entire wedding planning workshop. It's one very practical way to meet the needs of young adults who are making decisions that will affect the rest of their lives.

Plan a three- or four-hour event for a Saturday or Sunday afternoon or evening. Invite local bridal shops and wedding planning services to set up booths. Give a tour of your building, and highlight those areas of interest for those getting married. Have drawings for things like a wedding planning book, a nice unity candle, or a free floral arrangement.

Have those in attendance meet your pastor or pastoral staff or a counselor with experience in premarital counseling. You could even offer a couple half-hour sessions for them to answer questions about wedding and marriage preparation. They might also want to talk about the premarital counseling they offer and what is included, and they might want to lead the group in any sample exercises, such as communication activities.

The pastor or counselor should address the practical issues every young couple needs to think about—money, children, in-laws, sex, and dealing with conflict. Schedule 10- to 15-minute breaks between each session and a half-hour open forum at the end for couples to ask questions of your experts and discuss these topics with each other.

Another good idea would be to hold an open question-and-answer time with couples in your church who *have* happy marriages—from recent newlyweds to those who've been married 25 years or more. Also ask your couples to share 10 tips that have made their marriages successful.

Provide theme-related snacks for the event, such as wedding reception-type cake and punch. Or keep things simple with snacks like a box of chocolates, heart-shaped sugar cookies, or conversation heart candies. Give those supplying the food permission to be creative.

Promote your workshop on the page of your local newspaper where weddings are announced, as well as through local bridal shops, florists, and wedding planning agencies. Also, be sure to have information on marriage- and wedding-related services available, and let couples know that they're welcome to speak to your pastor or church at any time.

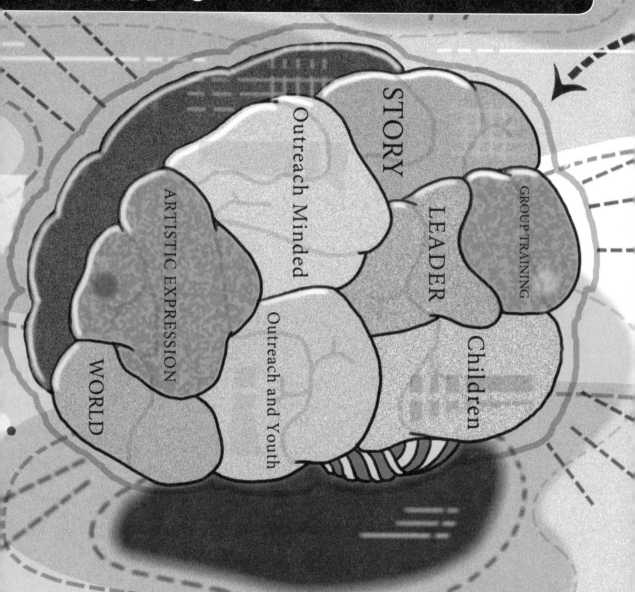

fig 1.1 **A Mind for Outreac**

WHETHER it's a one-time event or a long-term commitment, it's likely that the biggest obstacle to your church getting more involved in outreach is the statement "But I don't know *what* to do."

Sometimes that statement is caused by a lack of knowledge or experience with the *how*s of outreach. Just as often, though, individual Christians, groups, and churches are so overwhelmed by the number of needs out there that the real problem is deciding on *whom* and *where* to focus their attention.

And some may even need a little more help understanding the *why*—or, at least, in seeing that they're a part of the solution, too.

The ideas in this section will help your church— as well as smaller groups of all ages—sort out the *who, what, where, when, why,* and *how* of outreach and help you start getting it done. As you try these suggestions out for yourself, you and your church will gain focus and skills as well as better see the need for reaching out to your world for Jesus— very possibly in ways you'd never thought of before.

5 Ideas to Get Children and Youth Into Outreach

Idea 1   Welcome Wagon

Each month, new families relocate to your community. And with these families, there are children (and parents) who have to start all over in finding new friendships. Your kids can help make that transition a little easier and learn more about others' needs in doing so.

Have your children's or youth group create gift boxes for children moving into the area. Decide in advance what age range of kids you'll be making these for, then go for it!

Your boxes don't have to be extravagant, but they do need to be useful. Consider including any or all of the following: snacks, comic books, a list of your group's favorite places to visit (parks, skating rinks, music stores, ice cream places, and other hangouts), school supplies, inexpensive toys, or invitations for your church's children's programming.

You could even include small gift certificates for some of your favorite places. You could also give realtors coupons to pass to families moving into the area, which would be redeemable for a kid's gift box when the family visits your church.

This is also a great time to make the importance of reaching out to others as Jesus would become real to your kids. Here are a few questions to help your group debrief as they work on these gift boxes:

- How would you feel if you were moving from one city to another?

- Is it easy or hard to include a new child/teenager in playing with the friends you already have? Why?

- What can you do to help a new child/teenager who's feeling lonely?

Idea 2   Teacher Appreciation

In many places, public school teachers are still underpaid; in many more, they're subjected regularly to the scrutiny of public opinion. So give your children a way to give their teachers an extra helping of Jesus' love, and let them know that they're appreciated.

You'll need: potting soil, glue, water, colored tissue paper (have different colors available), shallow bowls, clean mason jars, flower seeds, and sheets of paper to create greeting cards.

Here's how you do it:

1. Before the kids arrive, mix the water and glue into a runny solution in the shallow bowls. Tear the tissue paper into small pieces, and set them into easy-to-reach piles on the table.

2. Instruct the children to use the different-colored tissue papers to make a stained-glass pattern on the mason jars by dipping pieces of tissue paper in the glue/water mixture and placing them on the jar.

3. When the glue has dried, help the children fill each jar with soil, plant a flower seed, and water it.

4. Help the children decorate a greeting card. On the front face of the card, have them draw a picture of a flower. Have them write beneath it, "Thanks for helping me grow in wisdom."

On the inside of the card, have them write the following Scripture passage, "Jesus grew in wisdom and in stature and in favor with God and all the people" (Luke 2:52), then sign their cards.

This cute craft will serve as a simple affirmation and let these public servants know how much they matter to your kids—and your church.

Idea 3   Group-Home Play Date

Chances are you have at least one group home or residential treatment center in your area that meets the needs of children with mental health issues. The children in these facilities deal with the frustration of not being able to live with their families, and their special needs make it difficult for them to build friendships with other children.

Reach out to these children by contacting their staff and scheduling play dates. You can schedule regular times for your children and the children from the group home to get together to play board games, play sports, or watch a movie together. You can also plan activities in the community such as skating parties, sled riding, or just meeting together at a playground.

You'll need to be mindful of a few things. Many treatment centers are regulated by a set of hospital standards that prohibit your children from visiting the children on their grounds. It will also be very difficult to get the approval for these activities to take place at someone's home from within your church. So

RECOMMENDED RESOURCE:

One great VBS program is Group's Galilee By-the-Sea, which transports kids back in time to experience actual biblical traditions—and to discover the truth about the man named Jesus.

you will need to either open up your church or find a neutral place where you can host these play dates.

Know also that many of these children have difficulty managing their frustrations and may use crude language or swear when they are angry. Coach your children and volunteers to ignore this language, and allow staff from the agency to deal with any issues. Point out that these children are important to Jesus and that Jesus loves us even when we do wrong things.

After your first experience, use these questions to help your kids learn from this outreach event:

- Was it easy or hard for you to meet new children? Why?
- How did you feel after the event?
- Why is it important for us to reach out and make new friends?

Once you've established a relationship with the children and staff at the group home, take more steps to grow your new friendships.

One idea would be to invite the children to your vacation Bible school. Many VBS programs organize children into small groups, which would be ideal for your group-home kids. Give their staff an orientation to your program and staff T-shirts. They can serve as small-group leaders for their own children.

Also invite the children to participate in your Sunday school classes. Encourage their staff to come and serve as aides. Many facilities are open to allowing their children to be involved in religious services as a way to demonstrate sensitivity to the children's cultural backgrounds.

Over time, the children will look forward to your visits, and you'll be an important part of their lives—and the staff's as well.

Idea 4   Empty Pockets Night

Generous giving as a reflection of Jesus' love is an essential part of spiritual training. As we give of our own resources, we also begin to appreciate and develop other ways to reach out to those who need it.

Together, find ways to give generously, cheerfully, and visibly. Choose a project where your youth group will give out of what they have and also become involved with people beyond just sending money.

Ask your youth group: "Would you be willing to give whatever is in your pockets for people who have nothing in their pockets?" (If some of the answers are "no," determine what those kids are *willing* to give. Try to keep everyone participating at every stage.)

Once you find out who's in—and hopefully, that will be your entire group—discuss what you want to do with the money you've just pooled together. Are there homeless in your neighborhood, women living in a nearby shelter, or…? If you can follow through that evening, do it. If not, make plans to do it the next time you get together, and be sure to do it as a group.

After your experience, discuss these questions:

- How difficult or easy is it for you to give generously? Why?
- Is it easier to give in some situations than in others? Which ones? Why?
- How does giving generously to others reflect Jesus' love?
- What other things can you do to train yourself to reflect Jesus' love every day?

Idea 5   Love Stinks

Use the relationships already existing within your youth group to open their eyes to what it means to take risks in friendship and treat others as Jesus did.

Set out a basin of water and a towel (have extras available for a larger group), and have everyone sit in a circle. (Even if they've figured it out, don't discuss why there's a basin and a towel in the middle of your group just yet.) Have students share their different perspectives on how well the members of your group know and treat one another. Ask:

- How well do you think we know one another? Give examples. What's something we can do to get to know one another better?

- How well do you think we *treat* one another? Give examples. What's one way we could treat each other better?

Listen for specific answers, and cue in on answers that touch on the idea of taking risks. Remind the group that risk-taking—and sometimes pushing others out of their comfort zones—was something Jesus did all the time!

With that, ask everyone in your group to take off their shoes and socks. Set the tone by kneeling before one of your group members and asking, "May I wash your feet?" If he or she gives permission, proceed to dip his or her feet in the water and wipe them dry.

Ask everyone else to follow your lead, and wash the feet of another person in the group. Continue in silence until everyone has had the opportunity to wash someone's feet and have his or her own feet washed, then ask:

- What were you thinking or feeling as you washed the other person's feet? as your own feet were being washed? Which was tougher, and why?

Have a volunteer read John 13:1-17 aloud, then discuss the following:

- What do you think the purpose was of what Jesus was doing?

- Besides washing feet, in what ways can you take a risk to treat someone the way Jesus would?

- What kinds of risks can we take as a group to reach out to others and treat them as Jesus would? Whom would you specifically like help reaching out to?

8 Ideas to Get Adult Groups Outreach-Minded

Idea 1   A (Personal) History Lesson

Sometimes the best way to get motivated to reach out to others is to remember how others reached out to us and to acknowledge the difference it made in our lives. Remembering our own needs and how God used others to meet them will reinvigorate our own desire and conviction to do the same for others.

Have your small group get together and spend an evening remembering the people who reached out and affected the course of your lives, whether they were parents, teachers, strangers, neighbors. Perhaps you had a co-worker who was always kind and willing to listen no matter what, a neighbor who was always willing to lend a helping hand, or someone on the street who simply handed you a Bible or gave you a scrap of hope or kindness. Select a few people who had an especially important or memorable effect on your life, and tell the group about them. Write their names down, and jot down what they did and how their actions—even the small ones—were important to you.

Another great idea is to ask group members to draw a timeline reflecting their personal stories and the key people who influenced them. Have the group consider how their timelines might have gone if those people were left out. Take time to acknowledge and give thanks for how God used each person in your lives.

Next, have everyone consider in what ways they're now able to reach out to others as others reached out to them. Think about how you could affect the course of another's life, taking cues from those who affected you. Have everyone try to come up with at least one idea they can take home and put into practice.

Check back with the group regularly, and find out how everyone is doing in their attempt. Also, consider repeating this exercise yearly, so newcomers can become more outreach-focused as well. It will also help those you've already worked with to see the progress they've made in people's lives and who has helped *them.*

Idea 2   Road Trip!

Stop trying to get new people to come to your small group. Instead, take your small group to *them,* and gain a better sense of what else God may want you to do in reaching out as a group.

Have a traveling group study that meets in different public places each week—high-traffic places where your group is sure to be noticed. Assign people to be "greeters," on the lookout for anyone who seems interested in what's going on. Have your greeters go introduce themselves and invite newcomers to join the group. Allow newcomers to "sit in" for a shorter period of time, if they prefer.

Brainstorm locations in advance, and think of various scenarios to make these locations work. These might include the local coffee shop, town center, or even the lounge area of a college dormitory.

Once your group gets past its initial discomfort, the variety will make meetings fun and help group members feel more empowered to share their faith with those they don't know as well. It will also help you to introduce yourself to people in the community and make it less threatening for those who may find it intimidating to walk through church doors.

Idea 3   Follow the Leader

Half the battle of learning to reach out to others is learning to obey God and step out when the opportunity arrives. Here's one exercise you can do to bring that idea home for your group.

Go for a walk or a hike in unfamiliar territory. Let each member of the group take turns leading the hike, and allow the person leading to make the decisions that need to be made as your group continues on hiking. (Of course, keep a trail map handy in case you *really* need it.)

Once you reach your destination (or at least after everyone's had a turn!), discuss the following questions:

• What was it like to lead the group into unfamiliar territory? to follow someone *else* into unfamiliar territory? Which was more difficult, and why?

- If you made a decision that affected the course of the hike, what did that feel like, and how did it affect the rest of the group?

- How is this hike like following God's promptings to "blaze a new trail" and reach out to someone else? When has God done that in your own life? What was the result?

- Why is it important to remember that God is leading and not just people?

- Whom might God be leading you to reach out to right now? How can we walk alongside and support you as God leads you there?

Idea 4   What're You Gonna Pick? Hot Topics!

If we're going to share Jesus with others, it's inevitable that we're going to get into discussions on topics where Christians and non-Christians disagree. Why not give your church some experience by having those discussions on "safer ground"?

Schedule a monthly Hot Topics Night where your church or group can discuss controversial topics with theological implications such as premarital sex, abortion, the supernatural, and capital punishment. In addition to the opportunity for outreach, this event will challenge those already in your church or group to think through their own positions and clarify what the Bible has to say about these controversial issues.

You could also consider meeting away from church, though, either in a member's home or at a local coffee shop or bookstore. Announce each month's topic in advance so members of your church can mention it when they invite others. Put up fliers in the place you'll be meeting so others can drop in, too.

Before your meeting, prepare a worksheet that discussion groups can use. Include several open-ended questions and a list of relevant Bible verses. Two books that can help you get started on ideas are *20 Hot Potatoes Christians Are Afraid to Touch* by Tony Campolo (W Publishing Group) and *Hot Topics, Tough Questions* by Bill Myers (Bethany House).

When everyone arrives for the discussion, form groups of four or five, keeping at least one of your "trainees" in each smaller group. Provide worksheets and extra Bibles. Designate one person as the discussion facilitator to ensure that each person gets to speak and to keep the discussion moving.

Your leader can walk around the room, listen to the various conversations, and remind groups to stay on the topic and on time. Because these are "hot" topics, the leader can also step in to prevent any discussion from getting *too* heated. If you see a disagreement growing out of hand, act as neutral facilitator, asking each person to outline his or her position without personal attack. You might need to recommend that they move on to the next question on the list.

Call the smaller groups together 15 minutes before the scheduled end of the meeting to allow some time for visiting and/or cooling down. Thank participants for coming, and allow those who need to leave to do so. If anyone wants to engage in more discussion, invite them to form one group or talk with you at another time.

Before anyone leaves, be sure to announce the time and topic of your next meeting. As everyone grows more comfortable with the format, you may be able to let the discussions become less formal.

Idea 5   Artistic Expression

Not all faith-sharing is verbal. And, contrary to beliefs in some circles, not all art is purely humanistic—although the church has often been in retreat in matters of the arts. The fact is, there are centuries' worth of art that has given both a positive and creative expression of God's love and glory. Take a night to open your group's eyes to the possibilities of expressing the love of God in new and creative ways, and use the visual arts to get your group started.

Encourage group members to bring examples of their favorite or best-known works of Christian art from throughout history. If some in your group aren't art aficionados, they can find many works of art on the Internet. Familiar examples would include Michelangelo's creation paintings from the Sistine Chapel, the rose windows of the Notre Dame Cathedral, and Leonardo da Vinci's *The Last Supper*. Ask group members to each bring at least one image (a color printout, a book, or a poster). Try to find more contemporary examples of Christian art as well—Christians in the Visual Arts (www.civa.org) is a good place to start.

Study Philippians 2:1-11. This is believed to be one of the early church's hymns. Then discuss the following:

- What images or themes seem to be most important to the early church? Why do you think this was?

- Which images seem especially relevant today? Which ones do you think are harder to grasp today? Why?

Now, share your art examples, and discuss the following questions:

- What images or themes of faith have been the most important through history? What do you think makes them so important?

- What themes are most important to your group right now?

- What biblical images do you think would be most relevant to those who don't know Jesus?

- If you or your group could create your own work of Christian art, what would it look like? How might members of this group or other Christian artists creatively portray it so a new generation could look at it with fresh eyes?

You could use this night to begin planning an art-based outreach by your church. Several communities sponsor art walks or "nights on the town"—leverage that by having your own display, with entertainment and refreshments at your church (or at a place you can use near the middle of town that evening). You could even open your own small gallery near the entrance of your church and show through your own creations the glory of *the* Creator.

Idea 6   Intergenerational Friendships

Teach your seniors and teens how to do outreach at the same time—by getting them to reach out to each other. Recognize the value of young and old having positive experiences together, and get them working together as they come to a better understanding of one another.

Begin connecting your seniors with children or youth *inside* the church with a prayer project, then move outside the church with other projects.

One idea, used by Cordova Neighborhood Church in Rancho Cordova, California, is to develop a prayer project that encourages seniors and teens to pray for one another. You can start this off slowly—get prayer requests from a few willing senior adults, and exchange them with requests from your junior or senior high groups.

After a few weeks, check your calendars for opportunities when your youth and seniors can spend regular time together, individually or as a group. Establish a simple schedule of sharing that includes questions asked by one group and time for responses by the other group.

Once you've established a comfort factor between the generations within your own church, start coming up with ways you can take this outside the church.

Idea 7   Q & A Night

Another idea to bring the generations together is to have a "Q & A Night." High school or college students, or those from a newlywed class or college and careers group, could meet with a group of older adults or seniors.

Come up with some discussion topics and questions. Imagine a high school or college student hearing a couple talk about how they kept their marriage together for more than 55 years or how *someone else's* parents have coped with teenagers or other conflicts. That alone could be an amazing insight for today's youth. By the same token, parents and seniors hearing high school students talk about some of the pressures they face today could be quite insightful.

As each side gains understanding of the other, this will also open the doors to mentoring or other ministry possibilities both inside and outside your church.

Idea 8   Spiritual Talent Search

Sometimes we don't reach out to others because we don't realize how much we really have to offer or because we don't know how to use what we have. Everyone has some talent or ability he or she would (or do) love to exercise, and pretty much any of those talents could be turned into an opportunity for outreach. How could those talents be used for God?

Have your small group hold a "talent night." Not everyone has the same or equal talents, but everyone can learn to use them to multiply the kingdom of God. Explore this subject. Consider taking a spiritual gifts test beforehand. Talk about hobbies, abilities, and opportunities. Try to go beyond pigeonholes for serving in a church, and focus on what gifts and opportunities God has given each person in his or her life as a whole.

One question that will almost always get people thinking is, "If you could do any kind of ministry (or could help people in any way) you wanted and knew you couldn't fail, what would you do?" Let your group dream big—we serve a big God.

Allow your group to start small as well, though. Help one another brainstorm ideas. Maybe someone has a special talent for cooking; he or she could make meals for the sick or overworked mothers. Perhaps someone works with people who have a rough home or family situation—could he or she invite people over for dinner? Maybe someone has an excellent education—what about a free tutoring service? Maybe someone has been gifted with great financial success— why not fund a food stand in the summer where poor people can buy fresh food at subsidized prices?

It's even possible that your small group has something in common, such as a gift for music, and could put on a series of concerts for the community. These are just some examples. Try to draw out what everyone enjoys, what they can do that they aren't doing but wish they were, and what special situations they're in. Once you have some ideas, make a commitment to pray for one another and support one another. If someone's talents would be useful in a church ministry, and it doesn't exist, start it, or help someone else start it.

Having people recognize their abilities and opportunities—and having the prayer, support, and encouragement of others in the use of those abilities—can push us to give what we have. Whereas before they might not have understood their gifts or been confident enough to pursue them, a meeting like this might provide exactly what they need to take the next step.

7 Ideas for Training Larger Groups

 ## Idea 1   Molding a Vision

One way to reach today's generations spiritually is to turn ordinary meetings into experiences. One key to doing this is getting people involved in your lesson or meeting.

Here's one idea: When people enter the room for your training session, give each of them a piece of modeling clay. As you open the session, ask the attendees to think about a prayer need they have. Then have them shape something out of the clay that represents that need. Encourage them to place the clay in an area where it will frequently remind them to pray.

Take it a step further, and ask your group to shape it into the first letter of the name of someone they'd like to reach for Christ. Whenever the person notices his or her clay letter, he or she can pray for that person. Or the prayer can use the clay to shape several letters for several names. The important thing is that your shape reminds the prayer to pray.

Also encourage your group to pray that God will open up ways for them to build a deeper relationship with those they're praying for, for their needs or situation, and that God will show them ways to get down to talking about Christ and the gospel.

 ## Idea 2   Telling Your Story

Another key way to reach today's generation is the power of story. When we share our stories, we also gain permission to introduce the author of that story—God. If you're trying to build relationships with others, it's important that you know how to clearly communicate the truth of the gospel in your own life to someone who has never heard it.

Prepare your own personal faith story to share with the group. Then guide group members through the process of telling their own stories. A clear, easy-to-share account consists of three parts: (1) what your life looked like before you trusted Jesus, (2) a clear explanation of how you chose to put your faith in Jesus (so others can follow and learn from your example), and (3) how your life has changed because of your relationship with Jesus.

For those who became Christians at an early age, the story might be a little different. They'll still want to share how they're growing in Jesus and how that's affected their lives and the decisions they've made.

Share your own faith story with the group, then hand out paper and pens, and give people 10 to 15 minutes to jot down notes about their own stories, hitting on the three points listed above as best they can.

Once group members have finished a rough draft, have them share their stories with people sitting near them. Pairs are best for the sake of time. For this meeting, ask everyone to go no longer than three minutes.

Listeners should keep their ears open for churchy words or phrases. For example, instead of saying "saved" or "accepted Christ," suggest "decided to follow Christ" or "decided to become a Christian." When the speaker has finished, have the listener share two or three good things about the person's presentation and one thing to work on. If the speaker went a lot longer than three minutes, help him or her think through what could be cut out to make the account shorter. Then switch roles.

Once everyone has shared, bring the whole group back together to talk about what they've learned. Encourage them to continue working on and perfecting their stories. The goal is not to put together a "perfect" story but one that's easy to share in conversation. To illustrate this point with your listeners, you can have them tell each other stories of how God has worked in their lives.

The important thing is that you learn to tell effective stories. Use details, characterization, humor, and emotion. Make it real to the listener. Leave out nothing. Hype it up. Use a little drama. Paint a scene. Help others to know Jesus the way *you* know him.

Idea 3　Helping Others Discover *Their* Stories

As you saw in our last idea, stories are powerful. They can spark abrupt laughter and bring the most stoic to tears. They are part of us. It's important for Christians to know and be able to tell their own story of how God has worked in their lives.

However, when *anyone* shares a story from his or her own life, it is because he or she trusts the hearer with the information. Creating a safe, welcoming relationship is key in sharing faith. Therefore, Christians should not only be good at *sharing* their stories but also at *hearing, listening to,* and *learning* the stories of others.

Train people to ask good questions and to hear the life stories of others. Good questions are personal. Good questions are natural. Good questions are in response to what someone is already telling you or to a shared experience. Good questions show people that they are cared about and that you want to hear them.

Instead of asking, "How was your vacation?" ask, "What was the most unforgettable part of your vacation? Why?" Instead of "How was your weekend?" ask whom they spent their time with and what they most enjoyed about those people. Being more intentional will show that you personally and specifically want to listen to others' stories.

You could even invite a guest to your group to share his or her personal story so the group can practice asking questions. You might bring in a single parent, a recovering alcoholic, a pregnant teenager, someone struggling with depression, or someone who's been seriously injured. Encourage your group to interview your visitor with whatever questions they'd like to ask. Afterward, ask:

- What did you learn from these stories?

- What does it mean to for us to "walk in someone else's shoes"?

- Now that we've heard these stories firsthand, what actions do you feel moved to take?

Encourage your church or group to take a fresh look at the people around them every day who don't have a relationship with God. Challenge them to pick one person and to pray for him or her every day. Also challenge them to learn the person's story—to ask questions, to share meals, to truly listen. This will open doors to share the gospel in ways that are personal and specific. Instead of giving information, it will bring God into the person's life in a way that has the most meaning and makes the most sense.

Idea 4   Stepping Out

God wants our stories—and others' stories—to be linked with his story. We need to learn the value of connecting to one another, even if it means getting out of our comfort zones to do it. The first step is always the hardest. So in order to share better with others how to connect with Jesus, have your group members take a closer look at the places where God has connected with *them*.

Break into subgroups, and discuss the following questions:

- Share about a time you felt close to God. What are some things you learned about God during that time?

- Now, share about a time when you felt distanced from God. What did God teach you during *that* time?

- Tell of a time you realized that God could meet the needs of someone you care about, and you were bold enough to present that to the other person.

Gather back together as a larger group, and share your answers. It might be a surprise—as well as a big relief—for many members of your group to realize that even those not-so-happy chapters of your stories are part of God's story.

Staying together as a larger group, discuss the following questions:

- As you look around your town and your world, what are some needs you see that you think Jesus probably wants something done about? How could you see God connecting to and meeting those needs?

- What gifts and abilities are represented in our group? Which local needs could they help meet?

- What are we going to decide to do?

Idea 5   Seeing Our Connections

There are a lot of different ways to categorize people. It can be an opportunity to pigeonhole others, or it can be an opportunity to discover connections that other people would overlook. Use the following exercise to discover how to link people together rather than divide them, and help your group gain understanding about how *they* can connect with those who don't know Jesus.

Ask group members to move about the room, and ask them to join into smaller groups, by any or all of the following groupings:

- gender
- rural/urban upbringing
- right-handed/left-handed
- only child/one of multiple children
- college major (such as arts and humanities, science and tech, no college, undecided)
- musical preference (country, rock 'n' roll, rap)
- those who pronounce the word *coupons* "coopons"/those who pronounce it "cyoopons"
- dog people/cat people/others
- people who grew up in a church/people who didn't
- any others you can think of

Go in whatever order you like, but after your final "reconnection," instruct your group to sit down in the subgroups they ended up with. Have them read Galatians 3:26-28 and discuss the following questions:

- As you look around your group, what kinds of groupings are represented? What human divisions aren't represented very well at all?
- What are some differences among people today that some think are too deep for God to heal?

Instruct each group to brainstorm for five minutes about how your group or church could become more representative of the larger culture around you. Get started by looking at different aspects of your current ministries.

- Small groups: What types of people are unlikely to get involved? What are some things we can do to change that?

- Large-group worship times: What can make our gatherings more welcoming to those who have differing viewpoints or backgrounds?

- Overall: What fears do we have about reaching out to others who are not like us? What can we gain by reaching out to them?

Outreach and inclusiveness are expressions of praise. What we really like, we tell others about. Close by asking God to give your group boldness to tell others about Jesus, and invite the group to worship God together with you.

Idea 6   Experiencing the Word

When we reach out to people today, we have to acknowledge— whether we like it or not—that they generally do not give the same value to the Bible's words as past generations did. Once upon a time, the Bible had an authoritative role in society, but in many societies today the Bible is not used as the standard of moral measurement. No longer does "It should be this way because the Bible says so" work.

As a result, faith has become much more experience oriented. Often not until someone experiences a point to be true will he or she choose to believe it. Help those who don't know Jesus to understand what your own experience has looked like, and help them to tie it back into God's unchanging Word.

Train your group to learn to share the truth of the Bible through the context of their lives and experiences, not just by quoting verses. As they learn to show how the Bible changed or affected or worked in their lives, they come across with more authority. The Bible was "real" to you in doing something good in your life; therefore, it could do the same in someone else's life as well.

Break into subgroups and let your members role-play. One person should try to share a truth from the Bible, while the other plays a person who doesn't support or believe in the Bible. Switch roles and try again. Point out to each other what worked and what could be done to make your sharing even more powerful.

By role-playing like this, leaders will get a taste of what it will be like to share their convictions with those who have yet to see the role God is already playing in their lives.

Idea 7   Prayer Walk

Sometimes the best way to discover what needs are in your community is to get out there and *look*. As we invite God to help us as we look, we can be confident that God will show us the needs he wants met.

Take your group for a prayer walk around your community. Pray for your neighborhood and the people you see in yards and houses, and say hello to neighbors and express an interest in their homes and lives.

Organize your prayer walk by neighborhood, letting church families from each neighborhood walk through their own their subdivision. In this way, there will be neighbors they know from past experiences or people they naturally would want to meet and introduce themselves to. While on the walk, members might greet people who are out cutting their lawns or sitting on a porch and introduce themselves and mention where they live. This will allow your group to be even more specific in their prayers for those families.

You could also prepare by making available a neighborhood map showing the names of people who live in the houses; your group members could use the map to pray specifically for those neighbors even if they don't actually see them on the prayer walk.

Plan to do your prayer walk once a week for several weeks, rather than just once or twice. This way, the walkers can get to know some of the neighbors and perhaps even share what they're doing and invite them to give their prayer requests so walkers can pray even more specifically. Follow up on those meetings by stopping by and asking if those neighbors have seen any results from the prayers.

From such contacts and efforts, your prayer-walk families can then invite neighbors to a local Bible study or to church events or do a service that would impact your community more greatly.

Bible Studies for People Who Don't Know the Bible

YOU want to reach out to others and show them Jesus. Therefore, you're also going to want to introduce them to God's Word and help them to understand that it *is* God's Word.

These five studies are designed to introduce those who don't know Jesus to the Bible and help them gain a better understanding of who Jesus really is. The activities are all developed so that they can be self-directed. There are times in each study, however, when the group leader is called upon, so be sure to read the study and be prepared to take the lead when necessary. Also be sure to gather all the supplies requested.

Plan for these Bible studies to last anywhere from 45 minutes to an hour and 15 minutes. Some groups will answer questions very quickly; others will spend more time on discussion because they're more comfortable with others in the group or just because they enjoy talking.

Feel free to adapt these studies to your group's needs. Add or delete questions or Scripture passages. Change the supplies or the prayer activity, if you need to. What's really important is that you enjoy these Bible studies and use them to help your group grow closer to God.

Study 1

Living an Upside-Down Life

Items Needed
- 1 pen or pencil for each person
- 1 piece of paper for each person

Opening (10-15 minutes)

Leader: Pass out pens/pencils and paper to each person.

Make a list of the things that people do to you that really irritate you or make you angry.

Pair up with another person, share your list, then answer the following questions:

- How do you respond when the things on your list happen to you?

- How do you feel about the responses you have?

- Is there anything you would like to do differently when people do these things?

Come back together as a larger group and share some of your answers from your pair-share time.

Bible Study (25-30 minutes)

Read Luke 6:27-36, then discuss the following.

- What is Jesus telling his listeners to do in this passage?

- What do you think this would mean to the Jews listening to Jesus who lived under the occupation and oppression of the Roman Empire at the time?

- Think of our society today. How do its pressures and values conflict with how Jesus teaches us to live in this passage?

- What's one way you can love your enemies as Jesus did, in a society that views "turning the other cheek" as weakness?

Closing (15-20 minutes)

Leader: Give another sheet of paper to each group member.

Break into groups of about four or five people. Make two columns on a piece of paper. Together, write in one column the things Jesus lists that others may do to you. In the second column, write the reaction to each that he calls us to. Then discuss the following:

- What do you find most challenging about responding to others as Jesus teaches in these verses?

- Who's someone you know (or have heard of) who has acted according to this standard that Jesus teaches? How did that person's actions stand out from what's considered "normal" behavior?

- What's one specific way that you can live day to day in this upside-down manner that Jesus teaches?

Leader: Close the Bible study time with prayer. Be sure to take time to ask everyone for individual prayer requests. Write these requests in the space below, and pray for everyone in your group.

Prayer Requests:

Study 2

The Love Connection

Items Needed

- 1 large piece of white poster board
- 1 package of fine-tip markers of various colors—enough for everyone in the group
- 1 piece of red 8 1/2 x 11 construction paper for each person
- 1 pair of scissors for each subgroup
- 1 roll of cellophane tape for each subgroup

Opening (10-15 minutes)

Leader: Tape your piece of poster board to the wall. At the top write the words "Love is…"

As a group, gather in front of your poster board. Everyone pick up the marker of your choice, and write as many ways you can think of to appropriately finish that sentence. Think of definitions from a variety of sources, such as lines from popular songs or movies, lines of poetry, Scripture or religious writings, or just popular sayings. Write them graffiti-style at various angles wherever they fit. Write as many as you like. The group should try to fill up the poster, if possible.

Afterward, discuss:

- Are there any common themes in the definitions that people wrote? What are they?

• What do these definitions say about the place of love in today's culture?

• Which ones do you see as most appropriate, from your own experience?

Bible Study (25-30 minutes)

Read 1 John 4:7-11, and then discuss:

• From what John writes here, what would he say was the best way to define what *real* love is? How is it like or unlike the phrases you just wrote?

• How should the idea that "God is love" affect the way we relate to God? the way we relate to others?

• Why do you think Jesus' sacrifice on the cross was such an important expression of God's love?

• Do you see the Christians around you faithfully proclaiming in word and deed that "God is love"? Give examples to support your position. How does that affect the way you think about Jesus?

- What would be the most important thing you would need to start doing (or do more often) in order to love the people around you in a way this passage calls for? How can you start doing it?

Closing (15-20 minutes)

Now, break into subgroups of three or four.

Leader: Give each person a piece of construction paper, and have him or her choose a marker. Also, give each subgroup a pair of scissors and a roll of tape. Ever heard of "wearing your heart on your sleeve"? In this activity, we are going to wear them on our *backs*.

Cut a heart out of your piece of construction paper. Make it as large as you can. Then have a member of your subgroup tape your heart to your back. Now go around the whole group and have people write on your heart one thing they perceive as being lovable about you.

After you've written on each person's heart, come back to your subgroup. Have someone help you take your hearts off your backs, then take a little time to read what others have written about you. Then discuss the following questions:

- What feelings did you experience when going around writing on each other's hearts? What feelings did you experience while reading what people had written?

- Why is affirming each other an important way to show love?

- How can we encourage each other to do other acts of love? What would most encourage *you*?

Come back together as a larger group, and discuss any highlights from your subgroup discussion.

Leader: Close the Bible study time with prayer. Be sure to take time to ask everyone for individual prayer requests. Write these requests in the space below, and pray for everyone in your group.

Prayer Requests:

Study 3

Jonah: After the Whale

Items Needed

• A current newspaper or newsmagazine for each subgroup

Opening (10-15 minutes)

Leader: Divide the group into smaller subgroups of three or four.

Think of a time in your life when someone showed you mercy, such as an undeserved or unexpected forgiveness. Then think of a time when someone refused to give you mercy, even after you offered a sincere apology. Share with others in your small group about these times, then discuss the following questions:

• What was it like to receive unexpected mercy?

• What did it feel like to have mercy denied?

• How did you respond to one or both situations? How does it affect you even today? Explain.

Bible Study (25-30 minutes)

Read chapters 3 and 4 of the book of Jonah. The events in these chapters come right after Jonah was spit out by the fish that God sent to save him from drowning.

- What kind of person do you think Jonah was? How would you describe his personality? What was good or bad about it?

- How would you describe *God's* behavior in these verses? Is there anything about God's response to Jonah that surprises you? Explain.

- In what ways did God have mercy on Jonah? (You may wish to refer to the first two chapters of Jonah.)

- What do you think God was trying to teach Jonah? Do you think he learned it? Why or why not?

- How do you react when someone who doesn't deserve mercy receives it? After reading this passage, what do you think God might say about it?

- What lesson is there in the story of Jonah for us today?

Closing (15-20 minutes)

Return to the subgroups formed in the opening exercise, then merge each group with one or two others to make larger subgroups.

Leader: Give each of the groups a few current newspapers or newsmagazines.

Look through the stories in the news articles, and find people who have done something wrong and deserve punishment. As you skim the stories, call out to each other whom you find and what his or her offense is. Once you have found several examples of misdeeds, answer the following questions.

- Do you think any of the individuals the group listed deserve mercy? Why or why not?

- Why do you think God wants to show mercy, and does, so often?

- Is there someone you have not yet shown mercy to? What do you think it will cost for you to do that? What's one thing you can do to begin to make that happen?

Leader: Close the Bible study time with prayer. Be sure to take time to ask everyone for individual prayer requests. Write these requests in the space below, and pray for everyone in your group.

Prayer Requests:

Study 4

American Idols

Items Needed
- 1 sheet of paper for each person in the group
- 1 pen or pencil for each person in the group
- 1 stick of modeling clay for each person in the group

Opening (10-15 minutes)

Leader: Give a sheet of paper and a pen or pencil to each group member.

Along the left-hand side of the paper, write the following time periods: "middle school," "high school," "college/early career," and "young adult." Leave some room between each entry.

Next to each time period, write down the name of one person you especially looked up to during that time period. It could be someone you knew personally or a famous person you admired. Also write down what it was about that person that made you look up to him or her.

Next, find a partner and compare what you have written about these "life heroes." Then, with this partner, discuss the following:

- What does whom we set up as heroes reveal about who we are and what we value?

- What is the difference, if any, between a "hero" and an "idol"?

Come back together as a larger group, and share highlights from your pair-share discussion.

Bible Study (25-30 minutes)

Read Acts 17:16-34, then discuss the following questions:

- How would you summarize Paul's reaction to the religious life of Athens? In what ways is it (and isn't it) like what we see among religions today?

- What did Paul point out as the main differences between the true God and the idols the Athenians worshipped (see verses 24-29)?

- Of all the things Paul taught about God, what do the Athenians seem to have the hardest time accepting? How is that similar to (or different from) today?

- If Paul is correct that God "is not far from any one of us," then why do so many have such a hard time finding him?

- Where are you in the process of finding God? In the midst of your search, what ideas or concepts about God have you had the hardest time wrapping your head around?

Closing (15-20 minutes)

Now break into subgroups of three or four.

Leader: Give each person a stick of modeling clay.
What are some things people hold in such high regard that they practically worship them? Choose one such person, thing, or experience that people treat as sacred, and use your modeling clay to make a statue symbolizing it. Share what you made, then discuss:

- How are these things that people worship today like the idols of Athens?

- How might worshipping people and things that *are not* God interfere with finding the one who *is* God?

- What would be the first step you should take in turning away from what you have treated like a god and toward the one who is the true God?

Come back together as a larger group, and discuss any highlights from your subgroup discussion.

Leader: Close the Bible study time with prayer. Be sure to take time to ask everyone for individual prayer requests. Write these requests in the space below, and pray for everyone in your group.

Prayer Requests:

Study 5

I've Got a Secret

Items Needed
- 1 piece of 8½ x 11 paper for each subgroup
- A selection of colored pens, pencils, or felt-tip markers for each subgroup

Opening (10-15 minutes)

Leader: Choose two group members ahead of time to come with a secret that no one else in the group would know about them. Tell them that the secret should be something that is interesting and something that would not be true of most people.

Divide your group in half.

Group members will play a short version of the classic television game show *I've Got a Secret*. Two people will share secrets. Half of the group will be the panel to ask questions of the first "guest," and half will be the panel to ask questions of the second "guest." As in the TV game show, each panelist will have 30 seconds to ask yes or no questions to help them determine what the guest's secret is. After each panelist finishes his or her series of questions, he or she can try to guess the secret. If no one guesses, the guest should reveal his or her secret.

After the game, discuss:
- What kinds of questions helped get at what the person's secret was, and what kinds of questions were not as helpful?

- Why is it fun to try to discover someone's secret?

Bible Study (25-30 minutes)

Read Matthew 16:13-20, and then discuss:
- What did Jesus want his disciples to keep secret (for the time being) from other people?

- Why do you think Jesus might have wanted to keep this as a secret at that point in time?

- Sometimes secular books and movies claim that certain "facts" about Jesus have been kept secret from the world by a church that sees them as scandalous (such as in *The Da Vinci Code*). Why are people attracted to allegedly scandalous secrets about Jesus?

  (Alternate: What are some other "secrets" about Jesus that you've heard about in the past [or recently, for that matter]? Or what are some other popular perceptions about Jesus that aren't biblical?)

- How did the way Peter saw Jesus differ from the popular perceptions of Jesus in his day?

- How does what Peter said about who Jesus is differ from secular perceptions today?

- If Jesus were to ask you, "But who do you say I am?" how would you answer?

Closing (15-20 minutes)

Now, break into subgroups of three or four.

Leader: Give each subgroup a piece of paper and a selection of colored pencils, pens, or felt-tip markers.

Have each subgroup determine who's the most artistic (or at least willing to draw!). With that person doing the drawing, the group should design what the home page of a Web site for Jesus Christ might look like. How would you describe Jesus to someone who does not know him? What graphics would you use? What links would you put on your site?

Take about five minutes to do this, and then discuss:

- How has people's understanding of who Jesus is become confused today?

- As your own perception of who Jesus is becomes clearer, how can you share that perception with others who are also seeking him?

Come back together as a larger group. Show the other subgroups your "home page," and discuss any highlights from your subgroup discussion.

Leader: Close the Bible study time with prayer. Be sure to take time to ask everyone for individual prayer requests. Write these requests in the space below, and pray for everyone in your group.

Prayer Requests:

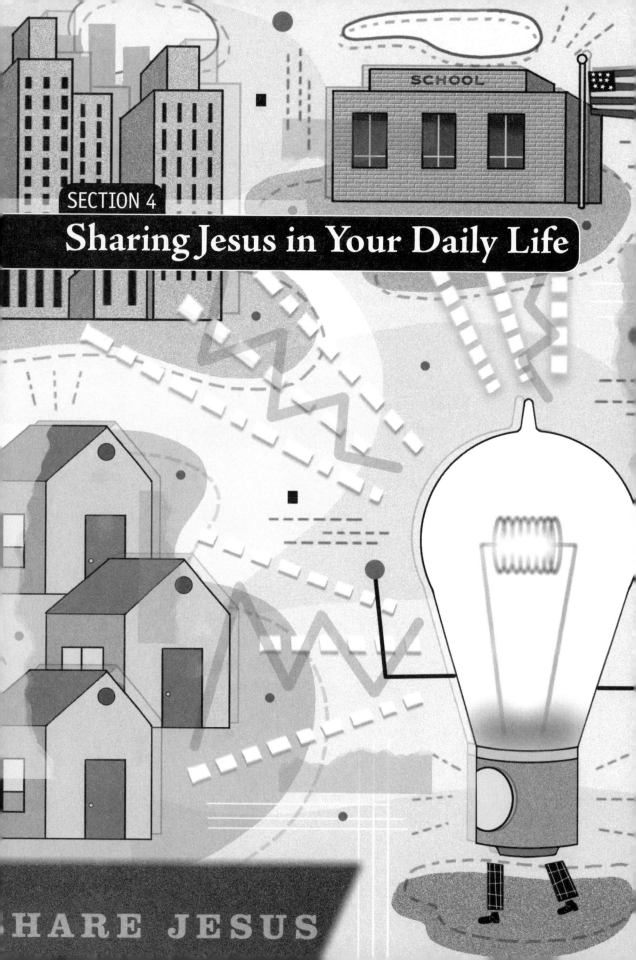

SECTION 4
Sharing Jesus in Your Daily Life

IF YOU haven't guessed by now, most of your church's outreach doesn't take place inside the church. (Well, it *shouldn't,* anyway.) What's more, a lot of outreach doesn't even fall under the category of "church events." Much of the real, rubber-hits-the-road sharing of Jesus takes place in our lives outside of church. In the schools. At our neighbors' house. While we're shopping or hanging out in the park. Or in that place many of us spend a great deal of our waking hours, the workplace.

Some of you are nodding your heads in agreement. Others of you are bristling with fear and self-consciousness. This section is for both of you—but especially the latter group.

The ideas in this section will help you to see that sharing Jesus in your daily life isn't difficult or scary. This section provides plenty of practical ways to get started doing it (or in taking the next step). So dive on in, and see what you can start using *right now*!

12 Ideas for Reaching Kids in Your Neighborhood

Idea 1   Home Is Where the Kids Are

Make your home a comfortable and inviting place for kids. This will make your own kids want to be there, they'll want to invite their friends over, and their friends will want to spend time at your house.

Dedicate a room in your home for kids to come visit. Try to have it a bit separated from normal house traffic so kids feel they have some privacy but so it's still accessible to parents. Set it up with a TV and DVD player, kid-friendly movies, possibly a gaming system, and some board games, along with comfortable couches and big floor pillows. The final touch is to keep a good supply of kid snacks in the house—chips, popcorn, frozen pizza, cheese, fruit, soda, and candy.

Now that you've got kids there, what do you do with them? Without intruding into "kid time," get to know them—start with simple yes-or-no questions, and show interest in their answers. The times you bring in munchies are good times for these casual conversations, as well as when they first show up at your house. It will take time, but show yourself to be a trusted adult. The kids will slowly open up to you, and you'll have opportunities to make a difference in their lives—whether it's about the heartbreak of a first crush or giving their hearts to Jesus.

Idea 2   Meet the Parents

With the scary news stories these days, neighborhood parents wisely won't let you do anything with their kids if they don't know you. So before you can reach out to the kids in your neighborhood, you'll need to reach out to the parents and establish at least a surface relationship with them. And, the fact is, you should.

Stop by and say hello when you see parents outside, invite their family over for a barbeque, or organize a block party to help you meet the families who live around you. You'll need to make multiple contacts with your neighbors to show that you genuinely care about them as people.

Once you've gotten to know families a bit, explain to the parents that you have a heart for kids, and tell them what kinds of activities you think you'll be doing. Give them your contact information, and let them know they're welcome to contact you at any time.

Idea 3   Kid Culture Crash Course

Culture is huge for kids. Their world is made up of all things on the Web, television, and other forms of entertainment. They live and breathe this stuff, so what better way to connect with kids than to be informed about the things that are important to them? Kids will respond to you if you can talk intelligently with them about the latest video game, the hot reality-TV show of the season, or the next Harry Potter book.

Use your knowledge of "kid stuff" to help you begin conversations with kids—whether it's just while you're saying "hi" to the neighbors or while you're involved in one of the other activities listed here.

Ask kids questions about the things in their culture—not "test questions," but ask what they thought about a certain movie or why characters did certain things. Kids need to know you care about things that are important to them before they'll care about the things that are important to you.

Idea 4   Start a Club

Find out what the kids in your neighborhood and your children's friends enjoy doing. It could be a sport such as skateboarding or basketball, or they may really be into video gaming or board games. Then set up an informal club or simply gather on a regular basis in the neighborhood to participate in the activity together, with you as the adult facilitator.

Be sure to get permission from each child's parent, especially if the kids will be meeting at your house. Invite kids to gather at the neighborhood park to teach each other sports skills. If it's a sport you know something about, give mini-clinics to pass on your skills. Weave in a few mentions about God while you build relationships with the kids—such as being thankful God made you tall so you can slam-dunk or mentioning the church league in which you play softball.

You can do the same thing with a hobby instead of a sport, too. Video games are a big draw for kids—set up a gaming club or tournament. Other ideas include crafts, books, or other skilled hobbies. Again, you can teach the kids what you know about the club topic; they'll also enjoy teaching you what they know if you show genuine interest in them. And along with casual mentions about your faith, the club will help you build relationships with kids that will "earn" you the right to talk about deeper faith issues with them.

Idea 5   Book 'Em!

By hosting a reading club, you can create a connection with the book-smart kids in your neighborhood. You'll also be letting your neighboring schools and parents know that you value children's intellectual development as well as their spiritual development.

Choose a book series that you believe will have a broad appeal to children in the community. Choose a time-honored classic, or consider visiting The New York Times best seller list to see what children are reading now. If you aren't familiar with a particular book, be sure to prescreen the book for any potentially objectionable content.

Consider hosting your club at a site outside of church, such as a public school, library, or bookstore. After acquiring the site and selecting the dates and times, be sure to advertise at locations where you'll find children readers and their parents.

Assign chapters for kids to read. During the week, read the chapters yourself, and prepare open-ended questions that will get the children talking. Be sure to ask questions that get children thinking about the ethical choices that characters are faced with. Make a note of any passages in the books that you would use to launch a faith discussion.

Once you have your book chosen, consider decorating your meeting space with themes from the book. For example, if you're reading a book about feudal knights or medieval times, you could paint a castle on a large appliance box. Or, if you're reading *Charlotte's Web,* consider making a large papier-mâché pig. Be creative and kids will become even more engaged in your book club.

At each session, serve snacks and lead off with the children sharing their favorite moments in the assigned reading. Next, transition into your discussion questions. Consider designing simple art, craft, or game activities themed to the book you are reading.

As the club progresses, be sure to have invitations to give the children, inviting them to other children's ministry events and your church's regular children's program.

Idea 6   Be a Volunteer

Your reach will probably extend a little further than your neighborhood when you get involved in local groups such as Boy and Girl Scouts or by being a sports coach—but it will also include kids that live near you. These groups put you in a position of being a mentor to young kids, where you can have a positive influence on their lives. Depending on the organization's rules, you may or may not be able to talk about God outright, but you can still show Jesus' love through your life. You could be the only adult in their lives who does.

You could also be a leader in a Christian group, such as Awana or Pioneer Clubs. Here you can encourage the kids in the group to bring their friends, giving you the opportunity to talk about Jesus to kids who may not otherwise hear the message.

Other options for volunteering with kids include helping with tutoring groups, participating in neighborhood schools as a teacher's aide, serving with parks and recreation departments, or getting involved with organizations such as Big Brothers Big Sisters of America.

Volunteering will help you develop relationships with kids, give you the time and place to talk to them about Jesus, and show them by your example the difference that God can make in their lives.

Idea 7   Sports Outreach

Recent studies show that childhood obesity and diabetes are on the rise in the United States. You can promote healthy lifestyles for children and build a relationship with your neighborhood by hosting a sports outreach program.

First, identify the athletes and coaches in your congregation. Determine what types of sports clinic you are able to offer: basketball, soccer, martial arts, or a general summer recreation program. Cast your vision to these sports-minded folks: They can connect neighborhood children to the church just by enjoying their sport! But don't forget to screen these volunteers with the same level of scrutiny that you would your Sunday school teachers. One great site where you can gain more information on guidelines, as well other volunteer ideas, is Church Volunteer Central (www.churchvolunteercentral.com).

Second, pick your location. Will you host the sports clinic at the church or at a local park? Do you have adequate facilities, or would you be better off renting a gym or a park?

Next, set the structure of the outreach. Will you offer a one-week half-day camp, or a five-week series of one-hour classes?

Also, make sure that your church has adequate levels of liability insurance. If you are renting a facility, you'll probably be asked to produce an insurance rider when you sign the contract. Your church's business administrator should be able to help you with this.

After you've picked your dates, be sure to heavily promote the event in your neighbor and community. Consider canvassing your neighborhood with fliers, using TV and radio public-service announcements, and working with your school district to have fliers sent home in children's book bags.

As you run the sports outreach, consider using some or all of these ways to build ongoing relationships between your church and the families you are serving:

- Send home invitations to your next children's ministry event, Sunday school program, or parenting class.

- Give the children screened water bottles or T-shirts with your logo on it.

- Create a database of names and addresses so you can invite the children to other ministry events at a later time.

Idea 8   After-School Pizza and Movie Party

Here's a fantastic way to expose children to Jesus and to meet the child-care needs of working parents. Arrange to get permission from several elementary schools to host a pizza party and a screening of *The Story of Jesus for Children* video. It's crucial that you are open with the administrator about your intentions. As long as your activity is voluntary, your schools are legally responsible to give religious groups the same access to the school that it gives any other group.

Create fliers to be sent home in every child's book bag. Again, show respect for parents by being open about the purpose of the event. Include a response form that includes a parental permission slip for the child to attend the party.

Prior to the event, purchase *The Story of Jesus for Children* on DVD at www.jesusfilmstore.com to send home with kids. You can also send the children home with Bibles—purchase inexpensive Bibles through your local Christian bookstore or at online stores such as www.biblesbythecase.com or www.cbd.com.

Use a video projector and portable public-address system to show the video. After the video, serve pizza and soda to the children. It's probably best to use the school cafeteria for the event in order to minimize cleanup.

When parents arrive send the children home with a copy of *The Story of Jesus for Children* DVD and a Bible. Be sure to include a bookmark that invites children to visit your church.

Idea 9   Choices Training

Each year, Greater Calvary Full Gospel Baptist Church in Erie, Pennsylvania, hosts an abstinence conference, which meets the needs of more than 700 children, teens, and parents in the community by providing education regarding drug abuse, tobacco, violence and bullying, and sexuality. Here's how you can host a similar event:

First, secure the usage of a large facility such as a public high school on a Saturday. For security purposes, it's best to obtain exclusive use of the building.

Second, recruit local experts from schools, churches, and local social-service agencies to present on each of the topics. Be sure to recruit presenters capable of reaching all of your targeted age groups—children, youth, and parents. Be very clear with your presenters regarding your expectations that all sex education be presented from the perspective of abstinence.

Promote the event through public schools, newspapers, and public-service announcements on television and radio. Be sure to contact service providers such as the YMCA, mental-health group homes, or residential treatment centers in order to invite the children they serve.

Also consider presenting the information concerning drugs, sex, and violence from a character base rather than a faith base. This will allow you to build bridges with social-service agencies and could even enable you to have access to grant monies to fund your event.

Here are some more field-tested tips that your church can use to make your conference a huge success:

- Explore grant-writing possibilities. You can write a grant that will bring in thousands of dollars to support your event and free up your budget for items to make your conference extra-special. Your church can then provide a free breakfast, lunch, and conference T-shirt for all participants.

- Host a free contemporary Christian concert. You can use it to kick off the conference or a closing rally at your church.

• Plan early. Start planning for your conference at least four months in advance. Coordinating this event is more involved than planning a vacation Bible school. Build separate teams for promotion, food service, security, setup and tear down, education, registration, and child care.

Idea 10   Respite Night

Special-needs children and their families are often alienated from churches because neither the children nor the parents feel that they fit in. And often, parents of special-needs children live with chronic exhaustion. Your church can offer an evening of child care for these children, so parents can go on a date, shop, or just go home and take a long nap.

Contact a local service provider that works with special-needs children, and present your intentions to offer a night of respite care at your church. Ask questions regarding the specific needs their children have. What volunteer-to-child ratio will you need to be aware of to recruit? What are the developmental and medical needs of the children? Will you need to recruit nurses to be on hand during the event? What activities will be both fun and developmentally appropriate? Are their any diet restrictions you need to be aware of?

The provider can help promote the evening to the parents that it services, usually through its parent support groups. You'll need to develop a registration form that includes emergency contact information and a description of the care that their child will need to receive that evening.

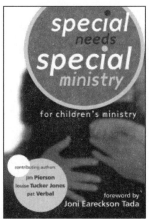

You'll find that recruiting can be a snap for this event. This is a great event to do in cooperation with your youth ministry. Over time, consider making this a monthly service that your church offers. As you build relationships with these parents, consider inviting them to budget training and marriage workshops that your church offers, as these are two areas of stress for parents of special-needs children.

RECOMMENDED RESOURCE:
For more help on ministering to special-needs children and their families, check out *Special Needs— Special Ministry* (Group).

Idea 11   VBS in the Park

Here's a thought: Why does vacation Bible school need to take place only within the walls of your church? Why not move your VBS program to a local park, where children already congregate during the summer months?

Contact your local government months in advance to secure permission to use a local park. Survey the park to see what types of activities will be conducive to the available spaces. Do you have enough room for large group games? for an opening and closing rally? Are there covered pavilions for snacking or crafts? The layout of the park will largely determine what activities you'll be able to do.

Next, purchase a VBS starter kit to use as a springboard for your programming. Since you're conducting this outdoors, you'll probably need to adapt the materials to meet your needs. As you design your VBS program, keep portability issues in mind. You'll want all of your daily supplies to fit in one or two pickup trucks or minivans. You'll need a portable public-address system. Consider purchasing several large plastic storage bins to transport your supplies.

Promote the event by passing out invitations in the neighborhood in the weeks leading up to the event. Consider purchasing large vinyl banners that you can hang at the park that will let passersby know what's happening.

Consider using a numbered wristband system for sign-ins and dismissal. Since you are going to be reaching families you aren't familiar with, it's important that you use a system that will ensure that you only dismiss children to the correct adult.

Have a rain plan. What will you do if you are rained out? Will you cancel the day or reschedule? If the weather looks "iffy," how will parents know whether or not the event will be canceled?

And finally, be prepared to offer "next steps" for these children and their families. At the closing day of VBS, you'll want to invite these families to your regular children's programming.

RECOMMENDED RESOURCE:

For an exciting VBS program about Jesus' love—filled with amazing adventures, unforgettable songs, memory-making crafts, and life-changing missions—check out Group's Avalanche Ranch: A Wild Ride Through God's Word.

Idea 12   Adopt a Fundraiser

It happens every year. Bombardment by children's groups engaged in fundraising—playgrounds, camp tuition, a special school trip. Instead of groaning then reluctantly writing a small check anyway, why not show Jesus' love by giving these fundraisers a *real* hand?

Contact the organizers of the fundraiser you're interesting in supporting, and offer to help them raise their money by hosting an event. Invite the fundraising organization to join with your children and parents as they put the event together. This is a great way help build friendships between your congregation and the community. Be sure to check with your church beforehand regarding its fundraising and funds-handling policy.

Emphasize to your participants that this event isn't primarily an occasion to share the gospel but an opportunity to build friendships—which, over time, will launch faith conversations.

There are plenty of great field-tested fundraising ideas you can use in your efforts to serve your community. Consider hosting a spaghetti dinner, pancake breakfast, aluminum recycling drive, garage sale, bike-a-thon, walk-a-thon…or any other "thon" your creative mind can come up with!

10 Ideas to Introduce Jesus to Your Friends

Idea 1   Seeds of Faith

There's nothing quite like a fresh salad made of veggies picked straight out of the garden—and it's even better to share the experience with a friend!

If you've got a neighbor whom you're trying to reach out to, consider planting a garden together in one of your backyards. Treat it as a team project, sharing the costs of soil and seeds and spending regular time together weeding and watering. And, of course, share the produce and enjoy it together. (Like most home gardeners, you'll probably *still* end up with a surplus of tomatoes and zucchini!)

As you and your neighbor work on your garden, use the time you spend together to get to know each other better and talk (as is befitting a garden conversation) about personal and spiritual *growth*. Have fun together using the garden as a metaphor for your conversations. You could ask questions like these:

- If our home life as children is like the soil we grow in, how did your "soil" influence the person you are today? Were there people who nurtured and cared for you? What "rocks" or "weeds" have attempted to hinder your growth?

- What positive events in your life were like nurturing water and sunlight, growing you into the person you are today?

- When have you grown most significantly in your life? How do you see yourself growing and changing right now? In what ways do you want to grow?

- What kinds of "fruit" do you most want to produce in your life? Why?

- Has faith, a belief in God, or some other spiritual practice influenced your personal growth? If so, how?

Be ready to share your own answers to these questions and, when appropriate, talk about the "seed" of faith planted in your own heart. If your friend is curious, invite him or her to read and talk about Jesus' parable of the sower in Luke 8:4-15.

Idea 2   Tasting the Word

Sharing meals together as Christians is a tradition that's been around since the days of the early church. However, it can also be a way to build relationships with friends and neighbors who *don't* know Jesus. Hold a fun one-time event, and if it goes really well, consider starting a regular gathering time.

Pick a cuisine, build an entire dinner and setting around your theme, and extend your invitations—in person, whenever possible. Extend your invitations two or three weeks in advance—far enough out that people have time to schedule, close enough that they remember to come and remain excited about the idea.

If you're doing this with other members of your church or small group, assign different parts of the meal to different group members, and give them fairly easy-to-follow but tasty recipes. (If your guests want to contribute as well, let them, but let them know up front that they're your guests and aren't obligated to do so.)

Be sure to not only have fun with the meal but with the atmosphere for each dinner. Find some music from the country or region whose food you're enjoying. Make or buy decorations that will remind you of that place.

Even more important than the foods you eat, though, are the relationships you grow. Take time to really listen to other friends, neighbors, or family members whom you invite to your meal. Don't force conversations; rather, take time for relationships to develop, and let them expand naturally while talking about work, the weekend, and anything else going on in each other's lives. And as needs are brought up, make a point of following up in prayer and by checking in with your friend or neighbor regularly to see how things are going.

Idea 3   Community Car Wash

Begin building relationships with your neighbors by offering a car wash on your corner or in front of your house. While cars are being washed, invite guests over for hot dogs, chips, and drinks. Talk to them. Find out their interests.

This is a fairly small window of opportunity for building a relationship, so think of it as a first step. Think of other community events you can offer right in your own neighborhood. You could even hitchhike on the idea and let the people who come watch a movie in your family room while the kids wash the cars.

Another approach would be to take a day to go from house to house and let your neighbors have a hand at washing *each other's* cars. Everyone can

have a hand in helping out. The more able among you can do oil changes
or radiator flushes, or at least check all the fluid levels (and take a run to the
auto shop if someone needs a top-off). Oil, transmission, brakes, steering, and
radiator are all possibilities, depending on the year and make of car.

As you go from house to house, use the opportunity to make a
conversational lunch and/or dinner out of it. With a little bit of advance
planning, you could arrange to have different foods and refreshments at each
home you stop at. Have a bigger celebration at your last stop, and take time to
appreciate the work you've done for each other.

The key here is that this is the beginning edge of a way to do outreach and
build relationships. You just want to arouse interest and be friendly. As you
get such efforts going, your neighbors will begin to see you and your family in
a different light. They'll begin to know what makes you tick and why you do
these things—and the Lord you do them for.

Idea 4   20 (or More) Questions

Canned evangelism "presentations" can be a real turnoff for spiritual
seekers. What most people long for—especially those interested in spiritual
things—is to talk openly and candidly about their thoughts, questions, and
ideas. All human beings are created by God and are made with a built-
in *longing* for God. Every single human experiences a profound spiritual
emptiness when living a life without Jesus!

In his book *Evangelism Outside the Box,* author Rick Richardson writes,
"We must challenge people today. We must ask them stimulating, intriguing,
even disturbing questions…[We must] bank on the fact that people have a
soul and spiritual interest and hunger…[We must] help people get in touch
with their longing, their yearning, their emptiness." You can naturally launch
meaningful spiritual discussions by asking your friends open-ended questions
that tap into those feelings of emptiness and yearning for God and for truth.

Dedicate some time to prayerfully creating a list of 20 (or more) questions
you could ask a friend or neighbor that will naturally open doors to more
meaningful discussions about spiritual things. You might want to include
questions like these:

- What do you think about [a tragic event in the news]? Do you think
  there is an ultimate meaning behind events like that?
- How do you go about teaching your kids about right and wrong? As a

parent, what do you use as a "compass" to guide your decisions?

- What was the best day in your life? What made that day so meaningful?
- Do you think people can really change? What about criminals or terrorists? What do you think are the underlying reasons for crime and violence?

The point here isn't to memorize your list of questions and then casually toss one out every time there is a break in the conversation; instead, consider this exercise as an opportunity to really connect with the thoughts and feelings of friends who don't know Jesus. Ask God to give you the boldness to take conversations to a deeper level—and be ready to share with your friends where you find your source of true meaning, purpose, and truth.

Idea 5   How-Do-You-Do Barbecue

Do you have some friends you've been reaching out to and wish you weren't doing it alone? Plan a small backyard cookout party at your house and invite them—and invite some Christian friends who can help you! It's one easy way to "network" your non-Christian friends into new friendships with other Christians!

Be intentional about inviting both friends who are Christian and those who aren't. Let your Christian friends know that you'd like them to be intentional about befriending your non-Christian guests, and ask them to join you in prayer about the event. Then plan a fun night, complete with backyard games (like volleyball or soccer for the kids), yummy food, and good music.

When your guests arrive, do your best to introduce people to each other and help launch conversations. Then sit back, relax, enjoy the time with your friends, and watch the Holy Spirit go to work!

Idea 6   Movie Time!

Nearly everyone likes a good movie. If your acquaintance and his or her family do, too, invite them over to enjoy a movie together. Spend time building relationships and finding out more about them, what they believe, what activities they're into.

For a listing of some movies that can naturally lead into conversations on spiritual subjects, check out Section 5 of this book, "20 Movie Nights," starting on page 114. After viewing the movie, raise some questions about the movie over a meal, snack, or ice cream.

Take it slow. Don't try to push people into a spiritual discussion they're not ready to have. At the same time, remember that most people have a spiritual interest, even if it isn't yet in Christianity. With the right questions, you can broach that interest in a way that leads to a deeper discussion about spiritual things.

Some people may think that if they don't become Christians, you'll reject them as friends. Make sure they know that's not the case. But also let them know you'll be praying for them and hoping for other opportunities to talk about the importance of your faith in your own life.

Idea 7   Out to Lunch

One of the simplest and best ways to show friends you care is to take them out to lunch. Find out who they are and what their ideas and dreams are. Talk about things of interest to *them,* and take the time to learn more about those subjects so you have more to say.

After having lunch a couple of times and maybe after other kinds of encounters, consider bringing Jesus into the conversation. After some small talk on the usual issues, bring up what you really want to say. Share what Jesus has done in your life and how he can do the same for your friend and whatever he or she is going through right now.

Assure your friend that you're not trying to judge or put him or her down. Rather, this is the most important thing in your life, and you, as a friend, feel it's something you have to share with everyone you know. Why? Because you don't want them to live their lives without knowing about the greatest gift in history. Put your friend at ease by being gentle and nonconfrontational about sin. And always use yourself as the example of the "worst of sinners," speaking clearly about the wrong things you have done, rather than pointing directly at him or her.

Have your Bible handy, preferably a pocket Bible or one in your briefcase. Let God open the door, then bring his Word into your conversation.

Idea 8   Seekers Study

There are many subjects seekers have interest in today, and offering a Bible study to some of your friends who are unchurched might be the ticket. You only need a few people for a study like this—maybe even just you and one other couple.

Share in the context of your home. Invite a couple in the neighborhood over for a study. Of course, you want to have built enough of a relationship with them to know their interests. In thinking about doing this, you might ask some leading questions: "Have you ever thought about sitting down and talking through some of the issues the Bible raises?" "If you could ask any question about Jesus or the Bible, what would it be?" Or, "How about sitting down with us some night and talking about spiritual things like the Bible? Would you be interested?"

(Some great interactive and introductory Bible studies can be found in Section 3, "Bible Studies for People Who Don't Know the Bible," starting on page 64.)

Often, it works well when such a study is offered in the context of your church, where you can get several couples or members involved who can turn around and invite people *they* know to your home study.

Have refreshments, too, and a very open atmosphere so people feel comfortable. If someone brings up an idea that goes against God's Word, couch your responses openly but not condemningly. Just stick to the facts. People will appreciate both your candor and your acceptance of them, and through your transparency they will catch a glimpse of who Jesus is.

Idea 9   Reality TV

Sometimes it can be difficult to invite unchurched friends to an event at church. They don't know most of the people, and they aren't familiar with the setting of your church. A more inviting setting can be a recurring event held at a home.

A fun event could be watching a reality-TV show together each week. Fans of these shows are going to watch them anyway, so why not watch them together and make it a fun event? (Use discretion in your choice of show, though.)

If you choose a show in which a contestant is "voted off" each week, make that part of the fun. Each person who attends could be assigned to one of the contestants, either randomly or by choice. Whoever gets voted off that week has to bring the refreshments next week! If you have a large number of people, two people can represent each TV contestant.

You can include regular members of your small group also, and encourage them to invite at least one friend who doesn't normally attend your group or church. The focus should be on friends who may not know Jesus personally yet or friends who are looking for a place to belong. A healthy mix of regulars and new people will help everyone feel more at ease.

Idea 10   Parent "Bridge Events"

One of the best ways to develop relationships for the kingdom of God is through your children. A natural outlet for you as parents is for your kids and others' kids to play together. That's a fertile ground for building relationships parent-to-parent, and it gives you plenty of time to simply relate to them and not turn everything into a gospel presentation. God will give you the opportunity you need to share your faith. In the meantime, spend time building trust and friendships so that you'll be encouraged to share when the time is right.

Also consider inviting a friend to a "bridge event" that gets him or her familiar with your church without forcing a commitment. Start with a family event like an Easter egg hunt at church. Make sure the event is a surefire fun thing for all concerned. In this way, you introduce your friends to a church context that is fun and ministers to their kids. That's important to parents. They could be drawn to your church and your Savior just through something like this, thinking that it would be a good place for their kids to learn some values.

If there's a gospel presentation at the event, let your friends know it up front so they're not surprised when things turn "religious." Most people will understand this and will be willing to go along. And if not, they'll probably tell you that, too. Give them permission to share whatever reservations they might have. Just accepting their concerns will convey Jesus' love to them.

19 Ways to Bring Jesus to Work

Idea 1   Joyful Noise

Don't know how to talk about Jesus at work? Then let your local Christian radio station or CD player do the talking, and in a way that co-workers can enjoy. Use music as a tool to share your faith in the workplace. Here are some ideas to get your thought processes going:

- Have CDs casually—or not so casually—displayed in your office. As others see them, they may express interest and want to borrow them. Let them.

- Check into getting Christian music on the company's "on-hold" system for incoming calls. Perhaps you can get a popular crossover group on the line, like Mercy Me. Or, considering the off-color banter of DJs that can happen even on easy-listening and oldies stations, encourage your boss to tune the on-hold system into a Christian music station.

- Have your favorite Christian music playing in the background in your cubicle. Be considerate—if others near you have a hard time concentrating with music going on, keep it low. And if someone doesn't like your selection, find one more compatible.

- If your office building keeps any background music playing, suggest Christian music. Praise music makes a great background selection.

- Do you have a group of people who do fitness at lunch? Bring along your boombox, and put on some of your favorite Christian music.

- When someone at the office celebrates a birthday, has a new baby, or even encounters a death in the family, include an appropriate Christian CD in the greeting card you send him or her.

With all of these ideas, exercise wisdom. Don't do anything that would adversely affect anyone else's job performance, including yours. And if someone tells you to turn it down (or even off), be considerate and do it—or at least switch to headphones.

Idea 2   "Working Out" Your Faith

Exercising is always more fun with a friend. Find a co-worker who enjoys the same type of exercise you do, and ask if he or she would like to work out with you. Working out together gives you several options of times to exercise—over lunch break or before or after work.

Use the time to develop a connection, share personal stories, and introduce your faith. You'll have more opportunity to do this with certain types of exercise, such as weight lifting, walking, or riding side-by-side stationary bicycles. If you're involved in a more vigorous sport that doesn't allow much time for talking, you can still use the time in the car or while you're taking a breather.

Don't push your beliefs on your co-worker, giving the impression that you have an ulterior motive for exercising together. Simply enjoy the time and build a friendship—where you naturally share the things that are important to you.

Another twist on this idea would be to exercise with a co-worker who's also a Christian. You can use the time to encourage each other in your faith walks, discuss issues related to your faith, or pray for each other while you work out.

Idea 3   A *Real* Workplace Mission Statement

You'll always act and respond better when you've thought things through and made a plan ahead of time. So think about how bringing Jesus to work would look in your specific job and for you personally.

How will you respond in certain situations? What lines will you draw? How overt will you be about what you believe? Write down everything you come up with, pray over the things you've written, and then boil them down into a one- or two-sentence mission statement for your life at work. Include how you'll deal with ethical issues specific to your job, what your priorities are, and what areas you absolutely won't compromise in.

To really make this meaningful, share your mission statement with a mentor or a good friend who will keep you accountable for following it. Your mission statement will keep you focused on living for Christ at work, and your life will speak louder than any words.

Idea 4   Sharing Your Faith—Legally

Have you ever started to share your faith while you're on the job and then wondered if it's legal—especially when someone else at work insists it's not?

The truth is, we actually have a lot of legal freedom when it comes to sharing our faith. Federal workers are protected by the Guidelines on Religious Exercise and Religious Expression in the Federal Workplace released in August 1997. Title VII of the 1964 Civil Rights Act, which says employers may not discriminate on the basis of race, gender, or religion, covers the rest of us.

What it boils down to is much like the Equal Access Act that is the rule in public schools. In the Equal Access ruling, Christian kids and clubs in schools are allowed the same rights and privileges as non-Christian kids and clubs. Likewise, in the workplace, an employer cannot stifle an employee's expression of faith, beyond the degree that they can stifle any other employee's opinions and personal expressions. For instance:

- You want to hang a poster in your office or put wallpaper on your computer that lists Scripture. That's fine—as long as other employees are allowed to put wallpaper on *their* computers or hang personal posters in *their* offices. If your co-worker can hang a surfing poster in his cubicle, you can hang a Jesus poster in yours. However, if the employer doesn't let other employees hang personal posters in their work spaces, you cannot hang a poster—religious or not.

- Can you use an empty boardroom for Bible studies during your lunchtime? Sure—if other employees are also allowed to use empty rooms for non-work purposes.

- The same is true for clothing. If anyone is allowed to wear a T-shirt of his or her choice, you can wear a religious T-shirt. If he or she is allowed to wear jewelry with the company uniform, you can wear religious jewelry. If only certain specified pieces are allowed (like only gold studs for earrings), then follow those rules.

- Are you allowed to verbally witness at work? The letter of the law gives a lot of freedom. We have a right to talk about our faith and to express it. On the other hand, we have to be considerate and should avoid questionable situations. We are free to talk about our faith at any time on our breaks, lunch hour, or before or after work. If we're allowed to talk about anything besides our job at various times during the day, we're also free to talk about our faith during those times. However, if we're witnessing when we should be working, employers have a right to ask us to focus on the job we're being paid for.

The force with which we share our faith can also be considered harassment.

Just as we expect our feelings, beliefs, and rights to be respected, we must respect others. If a co-worker asks us not to talk to him or her about the gospel, *honor that request*. Otherwise, that person is allowed to file a harassment complaint if we talk about faith to him or her again without permission.

So when it comes to sharing your faith at work, don't let your fears of legal limitations hinder you. The keys are to be respectful, sincere, and considerate. And isn't that what Jesus calls us to do, anyway?

Idea 5   **Lending Library**

Set up a small lending library in your work area. Include CDs of Christian music or books. Have a variety of music and literature on your shelves. If someone admires your taste in books or music, offer to let the person borrow the CD or book. If he or she *really* likes it, buy a copy for him or her. Consider it an investment in your friendship and in the kingdom of God.

If your company has the capacity (and you or someone you know has the technical know-how), you could also consider starting a shared office music file. Everyone in the office downloads their favorite songs into a folder or onto a CD or MP3 player. Keeping copyright laws in mind, pass around favorite songs—yours *and* theirs.

Idea 6   **Work Prayer**

Bringing Jesus to work isn't just about sharing your faith with co-workers. It's also about you and other Christians you work with supporting each other—being a visible presence to one another to remind yourselves that you're not alone.

If you know of other Christians in your office, set up a time to meet regularly for prayer, either over the lunch hour or before or after work. If your company will allow it, meet on-site; if not, look for a nearby coffee shop. It doesn't have to be a long meeting, but spend enough time for prayer requests to be shared and prayed over. The point is to support and encourage each other in your work, life, and Christian walk.

Spread the news of your meeting by word of mouth, or ask if you can put up notices on bulletin boards, put an announcement in a company newsletter, or send e-mail invitations to those who would be interested.

Pray for your co-workers who aren't part of the prayer meeting. If someone you work with is facing a difficult situation—whether it's a family crisis or even a tough meeting with the boss—ask if you can pray for, or with, him or her about it. Most people, even non-Christians, won't be offended by a genuine offer of prayer on their behalf. They may even admit they don't really know how to pray but would accept your prayers for them. Follow up later by saying, "I've been praying about your situation and wondered how things were going." Your care and attention will speak volumes about God's love.

Idea 7   Serve Your Co-Workers

Jesus practiced servant evangelism all the time—from washing his disciples' feet to offering a drink of water to a thirsty woman. Follow his example of love-in-action at work. There are many ways you could do this. Here are just 10 ideas to get you started.

- Offer your help to a co-worker who's buried under deadlines.
- Bring in a box of doughnuts for everyone to share—just because.
- Do the little things that no one else wants to do—cleaning the coffee pot, refilling the copier with paper or toner, emptying the recycling box.
- Give a co-worker a ride to work when his or her car is in the shop.
- Recognize special moments in the lives of those you work with—birthdays, weddings, big work anniversaries, promotions—with a card or personal note.
- Offer to cover for a co-worker during his or her vacation *before* you're asked.
- Buy a cup of coffee for your partner or secretary when you stop for one on the way to the office.
- Get to know your co-workers' interests outside of the office. Then do things that show you care enough to remember something that's important to them personally—forwarding a news story about their favorite hobby, telling them about a deal you found on tickets for their favorite team, or showing them an announcement about their favorite author giving a book signing.
- Invite someone you work with out to lunch, and pick up the tab.
- Volunteer your help with something outside of work—carrying moving boxes, hauling rocks, building a swing set, or doing some other multiperson job your co-worker mentions.

Caring for your co-workers shows them that Jesus isn't just someone you hear about in church, but he is someone whose life can be lived out wherever you are.

Idea 8   Get Out of the Workplace

When you're going to an event, invite a co-worker to go with you. The opportunities are endless—invite someone to lunch, to your church's cantata, to a ballgame, to a Christian businessperson's lunch, to a movie…anything to get together with him or her outside the workplace and develop a friendship.

Inviting a co-worker to do something with you brings Jesus to work in several ways. First, it allows you to share a part of your life that's not work-related with a co-worker, and second, it helps you develop and/or strengthen a friendship with that person. While you're out, you have the opportunity to have conversations about more personal things, including your faith.

Inviting a co-worker to an outside event shows you care about him or her in more ways than simply how he or she can help you do your job. An invitation can also provide opportunity to introduce him or her to other Christians who can have a positive impact by reflecting Jesus.

Idea 9   Being There

When a co-worker experiences a family loss, the birth of a child, a move, a surgery, or some other stress-filled life event, you can show God's love in a tangible way. Consider one of these ideas:

- Coordinate a schedule for others in your office to provide meals for the family.
- Bring his or her family a meal, but include some things others may not think of, like snacks and treats or a movie-rental or grocery-store gift card.
- Offer your help with things such as lawn care, baby-sitting, or errand-running.
- If money is needed—perhaps for health care—you could do something as simple as passing a jar around the office or something as elaborate as throwing a fundraiser.
- Send a card with a special message—maybe even one with a message of God's concern for the person as well during this time. Add a personal note as well.

Idea 10   Work Together—Away From Work

Is your company involved in a service project outside of the workplace? Get involved. Take the opportunity to get to know your co-workers in a totally different environment, and show Jesus' love to your co-workers and others while doing it.

Check with your human resources department or company secretary about programs your company is involved in, then pick one and get involved. Is it a reading program? a charity event? building a house for Habitat for Humanity? Be part of it. Are co-workers using some of their lunch hours to help at the urban day care? Go rock some babies with them.

This is a great opportunity to learn to reach out to others with the love of Jesus, and it will help you become more comfortable in doing so in a church context in the future as well. At the same time, you'll be able to show other co-workers you care by working with them and taking time to talk and listen as you do.

Idea 11   Book Club

Meet over lunch hour to discuss books that you all read together. Set it up so each person gets a chance to select a book that the group will read. When it's your turn, choose a Christian novel or narrative. Much Christian fiction gives a gospel presentation, or at least discusses the role of faith in life, giving you opportunity to discuss your own faith. Some novels by Christian authors also include group-discussion questions to help you lead the conversations.

Be sure the book you pick is quality literature. Christianity—and Christian books—should reflect God's excellence. For contemporary authors, take a look at selections from Walter Wangerin, Donald Miller, Robert Whitlow, Penelope Stokes, Dee Henderson, or Brock and Bodie Thoene, among others.

Allowing each member to choose a book for the group to read avoids the impression that you're just trying to "cram your views down the group's throat." However, realize that you'll need to be gracious about the books other group members select as well—even if they conflict with your beliefs. But bear in mind that it will give you the opportunity to share your faith and beliefs as you respond to the ideas in that book. You could even turn the tables by choosing a current hot book (such as *The Da Vinci Code*) and giving your views on it from a Christian perspective.

Idea 12   Jesus in the Work*space*

The way you decorate and live in your workspace reflects who you are. What do the things on your desk or in your cubicle say about you and what's important to you? If Jesus is a part of your life, do other people know that by looking around your work area?

You don't have to be obnoxious or pushy about your beliefs, but people want you to be authentic about who you really are. So be true to yourself and to Jesus with the way you design the space around you. Your work décor can be a silent witness for Jesus—whether it's a picture of you involved in a ministry, a poster of a Bible verse, or a cross with a special personal meaning. Be ready to explain each article's significance or why you're displaying it, in case someone asks. (See also Idea 4 in this section, "Sharing Your Faith— Legally," for more information about what's specifically permitted in the workplace.)

Another aspect to living as Jesus would in the workplace is how you act. Don't let your workspace and your behavior send conflicting messages about Jesus. Be sure your words, your actions, the way you treat others, and the way you do business is done as if you were working for the Lord—because you are.

Idea 13   News You Can Use

Current news events are always topics of discussion in the workplace. Get involved in these discussions, and give your co-workers a perspective they may not have considered. Here are some ways to work God's ideas into news or current-event discussions.

- When a big trial hits the news, share a Christian perspective on justice and compassion. Or you could mention how God rejects all sin, from the lies one tells to the murder a defendant is on trial for, and that's why we all need God's forgiveness and salvation.

- A story about people who are struggling with the effects of a natural disaster, who are hungry or sick, or who are oppressed under a corrupt government could give you the opportunity to talk about where God is during human suffering. You might even discuss ways to show the love of Jesus by actively supporting an organization addressing those issues.

- Discuss how God calls us to support our government leaders—even when we don't always agree with them—and to get involved in our community to make a difference.

As you bring a Christ-like perspective into current events, co-workers may also invite you to bring that perspective into their *personal* current events as well.

Idea 14 Getting Ready for Work—at Church

The workplace can be a tough place for a Christian—or a non-Christian, for that matter. Your church can be a place that acknowledges that fact and offers support for workers of all kinds.

Start a group that meets monthly to give support and ideas to folks who work in a secular environment. You could also set it up as a small group or Sunday school class. Use it as a way to equip workers with tools for bringing Jesus to work with them each day. This group can be a place of strengthening, emboldening, and empowering, so the workers can shine for Jesus during the week.

Here are some ideas to keep your group lively and relevant:

- Bring in Christian businesspeople as speakers to share how they live out their faith in the marketplace.

- Study together some of the many books on faith and work.

- Have a brainstorming session to come up with new ideas on how to live out your faith at work.

- Have discussions on work situations that are difficult as a Christian—such as being asked to do something unethical, dealing with workplace gossip and rumors, or being required to work on Sundays. Develop ways to help each other deal with these situations in a way that God would approve of.

Idea 15 The Word at Work

Consider starting a Bible study at your workplace. This can be a great way for Christians to reach out to co-workers who are interested in Christianity, as well as bond with any Christians who want to come.

The first step is to plan out what you'd like to do. If you know another Christian at work who would like to tackle the project with you, you might get together at lunch one day to discuss the idea.

How simple or complicated starting a Bible study is depends to some degree upon the people you work for. After you determine how you'd ideally like to have your Bible study, get permission from the administration to use an area of the building for this purpose—lunchroom, conference room, or wherever—during lunchtime or before work. You might even do some Internet research and pull together copies of published studies that show how much healthier people are when faith is part of their lives (interpretation: healthier employees can mean cheaper insurance premiums for employers), or how Christians are better workers. For examples of such studies, check out www .pewforum.org and www.gallup.com.

If the administration supports the idea of offering a Bible study group, put notices on the bulletin board or in the company newsletter. When you have your time and place set up—perhaps you'll want to have a Bible study once a week, or you might want to meet three times a week—start letting others know. Also, it's wise to have others from your church, or other Christian friends, praying with you about this outreach.

For curriculum, you can check out the Bible studies in this book (starting on page 64), check your local Christian bookstore, look on the Internet, or develop your own. You might also draw seekers if you have studies that tie into cultural topics.

If the administration at your workplace will allow you to use part of the building for this, remind all participants to be good employees by getting back to work on time. At all times, make sure people know this is employee-led and voluntary—never make it sound like a sanctioned or required event.

If your administration will not let you use the building, you can still have an employee Bible study. Simply meet at a restaurant or coffee shop near your work location. Have a definite beginning and ending time, and enjoy your time together!

Idea 16   Supernatural Nursing Care

Nurses and other hospital volunteers have a unique opportunity to offer touches of God's grace to co-workers, patients, and patients' families. If your workplace employs a chaplain, link hearts and start a weekly prayer meeting. Once you're known as the nurse or volunteer who prays, you'll also start receiving patients' names from your co-workers. Sacrificing a half-hour in prayer before your shift begins pays high dividends. You'll witness a variety of miracles and enjoy improved staff relationships.

To strengthen your outreach, network with your church's prayer team by sharing specific prayer requests, and keep requests updated and current. Your congregation can also show God's love through you by occasionally providing a spread of doughnuts and bagels for the doctors' or nurses' lounge room. By attaching a personal note of thanks and encouragement, you convey the message, "Jesus cares, and so do we!"

You can also extend Jesus' love in practical ways to other co-workers. Working 12-hour shifts causes added stress to nurses when trying to arrange rides for their kids to get to sports events or various appointments. By offering your church's volunteer list of names and phone numbers, you can help relieve your co-workers' burdens for child care. Also, if you have a masseur or masseuse in your church family, offer 15-minute neck or back massages, on-site, during break or lunch.

Your acts of mercy—offering help, hope, and comfort—are a surefire way to make the love of Jesus visible to both co-workers and patients!

Idea 17 **Welcome to Our Country!**

Our international population in the Unites States, whether here on work visa or otherwise, is increasing by the millions and populates all levels of the workplace. As they may be the only people you ever meet from their countries, you have a unique opportunity to show them who Jesus really is before they return to their countries. And there are some practical ways to show that you, and Jesus, care about them.

- Consider providing transportation to jobs, schools, or shopping.

- If they need help understanding the legal mumbo jumbo of a rental contract, offer assistance before they sign an agreement. If they come to America empty-handed, they'll need furniture, so give generously.

- Invite them to social events, such as family cookouts and recreational activities. Their social and emotional well-being will soar. It also gives opportunities for them to practice their English-language skills.

- Ask personal questions like, "Is your family here or still in your home country?" "Do you live alone?" "Do you have a spouse or children?" Learn to pronounce their native names correctly; it shows respect and honor.

- Internationals are usually curious and open to learning about American customs and traditions. Therefore, as holidays approach, invite them over, weaving your beliefs into your celebrations. For example, at Easter, emphasize the rebirth of plants with Jesus' death and resurrection.

No matter what your vocation, with acts of kindness coupled with prayer, internationals will be touched by Jesus' love.

Idea 18   Knowing When to Share

"Share your faith—share your faith—share your faith." You might not have been raised with that mantra, but still, most of us have an innate desire to share our faith with our co-workers. How can we do so, even for those of us to whom sharing our faith doesn't come naturally?

- **Pray.** Ask God to make you observant and to open doors. Ask God to help you be bold, yet sensitive.

- *Really* **listen.** Sometimes people drop hints that they want to talk about their faith, whatever their current understanding of faith may be. Listen and sense whether it's time to pursue it, and how. If a co-worker has just said something that's a clear lead-in for the gospel, but you feel the timing isn't right—perhaps the person is on a deadline or in a meeting— wait. Pray and make another opportunity to talk later. Lead by saying, "You know, I've been thinking about what you said."

- **Be prepared.** Think through situations and what you'd say. First Peter 3:15 tells us, "If someone asks about your Christian hope, always be ready to explain it." You could even gather some friends to role-play talking about your faith together.

- **Location is everything.** Your co-worker may be ready for the gospel, but probably not in front of others. So wisely choose *where* you share. Instead of the office cafeteria, go out to lunch. Find a neutral place where he or she won't feel intimidated or "set up."

- **Respect is vital.** Often people won't listen to our message if they think we're talking down to them. Think of what you admire about this person, and let your co-worker know it, too.

- **Know when it's time to stop.** We don't have to put a notch in our gospel belts of leading someone to Christ. If we just plant a seed that the Holy Spirit can bring to fruition, we may have succeeded in doing exactly what God wants us to do.

Idea 19   The Gift of Presence

It's often been said, "You never forget the people who attend your wedding or the funeral of someone you love," and those who have experienced either or both know the truth of those words. You always have a special feeling in your heart for those who were there for those important times.

As Christians, we have an opportunity to share the love of Jesus with those who really need to hear it on those and other special occasions. What are some of the functions where our presence can make a difference?

- **Those happy life moments.** Okay, so you hate baby showers; and if you eat one more piece of wedding cake in your life, you're afraid you'll barf. It may be old news and routine to you, but it is an important time in your co-worker's life. Pray for grace and be there, offering your support and best wishes.

- **Share the good times.** Your co-worker's daughter has the lead in the school musical, and your co-worker is so proud. Or your co-worker plays the guitar at a local coffeehouse. If you really want to make a statement, show up.

- **Party—even if not so hardy!** If there's an office party where you know alcohol will be served (and if you're comfortable doing it), go anyway, and refrain from joining in the drinking. It will show co-workers that you live your life a little differently, but it will also convey that you don't think you're too good to be with them.

- **And then there's the other side.** Very few people in this world are funeral crashers—instead, we try to think of any valid excuse we can to avoid looking death in the face. However, when our co-worker's loved one has died, he or she needs our love, concern, and faith. You can especially be used by God in the days immediately following the funeral—while the family is still flailing in shock (and often back in their own parts of the world). You can be a strong spiritual and personal presence who stays available.

Spending time with people—in good moments and bad—results in strong relationships. And those relationships are what lead to great opportunities to share Jesus.

20 Movie Nights

MOVIES get a bad rap in some church circles. But the fact is, they're often both moving and effective in portraying basic truths about us, both humanly and spiritually speaking, in ways that few sermons can. So why not leverage that by having a movie night together and drawing out the truths imbedded in those films?

Movie nights aren't just about watching movies. The point is to set up discussions and encourage fellowship—the movies are simply shared experiences and discussion prompts. Here are several ideas to ensure that the movies and the environment you select are appropriate:

1. *Meet in a home.* When people come into each other's homes, they form a natural bond.

2. *Serve movie food.* Popcorn, chips, pizza, candy, and soda will do it. Ask each group member to bring something to pass around. This ensures that you won't go broke, and it builds ownership of the event. (You *could* also tie in your food to the theme of your movie, if cost isn't as big of a factor.)

3. *Choose your movies wisely.* While the host can decide what to rent, the video or DVD should be less than two and a half hours long, thought provoking, and include substantial spiritual and/or emotional content. Also...

4. *Stick with PG or PG-13.* While there will almost always be something in a movie that could offend someone in your group, a PG rating usually ensures that the offense will be minor.

5. *Don't announce the movie's title beforehand.* Some people might decide not to attend because they've already seen the film. But remember, the movie itself isn't the point. Discussion and relationships matter more, so don't reveal the title until plates are full and people are already parked in front of the screen.

6. *The host controls the remote.* This is a matter of respect and resolves a battle before it ever starts.

7. *No pausing.* Once the movie starts, it keeps rolling. That means people need to plan ahead for bathroom breaks and refilling sodas. Why? If you stop any time someone needs to visit the little boys' or girls' room, you'll still be watching at breakfast the next day!

8. *The host starts the discussion.* After the movie ends, it's the host's job to get the conversation rolling. The discussion may suddenly take a dramatic turn once it starts, but the first nudge is up to the host.

9. *Keep this one to yourself:* A question that *always* works when the discussion is floundering is "Which character in this movie do you most closely identify with, and why?" Pull this question out only if the discussion screeches to a halt.

10. *Don't meet* too *often.* Keep your movie nights to every month or two. This will keep the event fresh and still allow you to maintain the relationships you're trying to build—especially if you do other activities together.

So have fun, and watch as the discussions—and friendships—go places you never expected!

Movie 1: *Good Night, and Good Luck* (2005)

Genre: Drama

Length: 93 minutes

Rating: PG for mild thematic elements and brief language

Plot: CBS journalist Edward R. Murrow and producer Fred Friendly take a stand against Senator Joseph McCarthy's anti-communist crusade in the 1950s. Murrow's broadcasts begin McCarthy's public and political downhill slide, but the battle inflicts wounds on both sides. The shows begin to alienate advertisers, and as CBS begins to lose profits, Murrow's boss finds himself caught between the need for integrity in television news and the need for corporate sponsorship.

Discussion Starter Questions:

• Do you agree with how Murrow and Friendly went about their job in this film? Explain.

• How do you explain the culture of fear that developed during the McCarthy era? What similarities, if any, do you see in our culture today?

• How do you think our society should respond to people whose values differ from ours? How should we respond as individuals?

• In your opinion, what is the responsibility of the media in our everyday lives? What impact does the media have on our way of thinking?

• What is the power of the spoken word in our world? How is it demonstrated in this film? How have you seen it demonstrated in your own life?

Movie 2: *Dreamer* (2005)

Genre: Drama/Family/ Sport

Length: 106 minutes

Rating: PG for brief mild language

Plot: This movie, "inspired" by a true story, focuses primarily on Ben Crane and his daughter, Cale. Ben trains racehorses and seldom has much time for his daughter, who loves horses herself. When something appears to be wrong with a prize filly before a race, Ben tells the owner not to race her. When he does and the filly falls and breaks her leg, the owner fires Ben and gives him the horse in lieu of wages. Against all odds, Ben and Cale, with the help of Ben's father, nurse the horse—and their own relationship—back to health.

Discussion Starter Questions:

- What was Cale's relationship with her father like at the beginning of the movie? What was it like at the end?

- What was Ben's relationship with his father like at the beginning of the movie? What was it like at the end?

- What caused the changes in these relationships?

- Describe a relationship in your own life where healing took place. What did it take for it to begin healing?

- What else can we learn from this movie about the importance of family?

Movie 3: *Walk the Line* (2005)

Genre: Drama

Length: 136 minutes

Rating: PG-13 for some language, thematic material, and depiction of drug dependency

Plot: Growing up in Arkansas, Johnny Cash had a close relationship with his older brother and an interest in music. But when his brother dies in a freak accident, Johnny develops a sense of guilt and deep pain from the loss. As soon as he's old enough, Johnny escapes into the Army, where he's able to travel, and he learns to play the guitar and experiment with songwriting.

When he returns to the States, he attempts to settle into a normal life. He marries, gets a job as a salesman, has kids, and forms a local band—which is discovered by the legendary Sam Phillips. He goes on several tours with Elvis and Jerry Lee Lewis, among others. It is not long, though, before Johnny's marriage falls apart.

During this time, he also meets and tours with his childhood idol June Carter. It is not until June and her devout Christian parents help Cash overcome his addictions that he slowly begins to straighten out the rest of his life.

Discussion Starter Questions:

- What particularly struck you about Johnny Cash's life? What aspects of the relationship between Johnny and June caught your attention? Why?

- How did Johnny's relationship with his dad impact him throughout his life? Is it possible for a person to find healing from such painful, dysfunctional relationships? Explain.

- Why do you think June Carter and her parents decided to help Johnny? What do you think motivated their kindness and commitment to him?

- Why do you think music was such an attraction for Cash? What is it about his music—or other music—that you find appealing?

Movie 4: *The Greatest Game Ever Played* (2005)

Genre: Drama/History/Sport

Length: 120 minutes

Rating: PG for some brief mild language

Plot: Based on a true story, 20-year-old caddy Francis Ouimet overcomes his father's opposition—and the mockery of the upper-class American golf establishment—to qualify for the 1913 U.S. Open Golf Championship.

His main challenge in his improbable quest for the championship comes from the world's reigning golf champion, the British (and also "lower-class") Harry Vardon, who faces huge amounts of pressure to win from the upper-class *British* golf establishment.

Discussion Starter Questions:

- What surprised you about the portrayal of the class systems in Britain and America—less than a century ago? Where do you still see different kinds of class systems today?

- Think of a time when you felt discriminated against or judged by others around you—for whatever reason. What happened? How did it make you feel?

- What did you think of Francis' father's actions? Why do you think he acted the way he did?

- In what ways did Francis show his father honor? Was Francis justified in eventually refusing to obey his father? Why or why not?

- How did Francis demonstrate persistence? Do you think you would've persisted as long as he did? Why or why not?

- What's one thing you're persevering with right now? What can you do—or who can help you—to persevere better in that situation?

Movie 5: *End of the Spear* (2006)

Genre: Drama

Length: 108 minutes

Rating: PG-13 for intense sequences of violence

Plot: *End of the Spear* is the true story of a group of five Christian missionaries, among them Jim Elliot and Nate Saint, who set out to reach the Waodani tribe in Ecuador in 1956 and paid for it with their lives.

It's also the story of how their wives and children later choose to go back into the jungle to minister to the Waodani—particularly to their leader, Mincayani, who was personally responsible for the murders. What results is a powerful, true-life illustration of the radical love of Jesus.

Discussion Starter Questions:

• What do you think of when you hear the word *missionary*? How was the portrayal here similar or different from what you pictured?

• Do you think it was right for the missionaries to tell the Waodani tribe that their culture was wrong? Why or why not?

• Why do you think God would allow his missionaries to be murdered? What's the incentive to be a missionary if God doesn't guarantee our personal protection?

• How do you see forgiveness portrayed in the film? Could you ever forgive in similar circumstances? Why or why not? Are there situations where a person is justified in *not* offering forgiveness? Explain.

• What's the purpose of forgiveness? How does it affect the person who was wronged? How does it affect the person who forgives?

• Is there a situation right now where you could use (or offer) forgiveness? What can you do that will help make that happen?

Movie 6: *Everything Is Illuminated* (2005)

Genre: Adventure/Comedy/Drama

Length: 106 minutes

Rating: PG-13 for some disturbing images/violence, sexual content, and
language

Plot: Jonathan is a quiet, large-spectacled Jewish American known as
"The Collector" because he accumulates bits and pieces of his life and stores
them in Ziploc bags. He goes on a search to find the woman who saved
his grandfather during World War II, in a Ukrainian village that had been
obliterated by the Nazis.

With the guide of a cranky grandfather and his overenthusiastic grandson
Alex—whose near-constant stream of twisted English only makes matters more
difficult—Jonathan begins his uncomfortable and annoying trek. But what
starts out as a farcical journey turns meaningful, as the past—and increasingly
astounding revelations about it—begins to emerge.

Discussion Starter Questions:

- What do you think Jonathan is really searching for? What are Alex and
  his grandfather searching for? What does each character find?

- What do you think of Alex's grandfather's attitude toward the Ukrainian
  Jews? What do you think fuels that attitude? How does it change as the
  movie progresses?

- How responsible are we for the evil that happens in the world? Should
  we feel guilty for others' actions—especially actions done by those we
  know personally? Why or why not?

- How does the humor in the movie make it more (or less) poignant, once
  the truth has been discovered? Did you find this movie more hopeful or
  tragic? Explain.

Movie 7: *Hotel Rwanda* (2004)

Genre: Drama

Length: 121 minutes

Rating: PG-13 for some violence, disturbing images, and brief strong language

Plot: This film is set in 1994 in Rwanda. People are trying to carry on with their lives the best they can in the midst of war and genocide, as more than 800,000 Rwandans die during the brutal three-month conflict between the Hutu and Tutsi ethnic groups. While trying to ensure the survival of himself and his family, hotel manager Paul Rusesabagina is caught in the middle. Somehow his hotel becomes a natural holding place for refugees trying to find shelter from the mass murder going on outside its walls.

Though resistant at first, Rusesabagina soon begins to see the importance of helping the people around him, even though his choice endangers both himself and his family.

Discussion Starter Questions:

- How was Paul Rusesabagina able to pull off his mission? What do you think are his reasons for doing so?

- Would you call Rusesabagina a hero? Why or why not?

- What do you think about the countries and leaders who stood by and let the tragedy happen without intervening? When is it OK for countries to get involved in other countries' business?

- What is our responsibility to our family? to society? What about when these two seemingly come into conflict?

- What is our responsibility toward the helpless of society? Who are the helpless *you* know of? What are some ways you might be able to get involved to help them?

Movie 8: *Crimes and Misdemeanors* (1989)

Genre: Comedy/Drama

Length: 107 minutes

Rating: PG-13 for language and some sexuality

Plot: Doctor Judah Rosenthal is a successful man—he has a good family and a respectable and profitable career. However, he is trapped in an ongoing affair with Dolores. When she gives him an ultimatum—marriage or full disclosure—he is faced with a crisis: He can do the right thing and come clean, risking his "perfect" life, or he can bury his dark secret in murder and go on living as if everything were normal.

Meanwhile, filmmaker Cliff Stern, whose marriage is also on the rocks, is forced into directing a film that goes against his artistic sensibilities. While his marriage and career are falling apart, he begins to pursue Halley Reed, a film producer. Both men face desperation but address their problems in very different ways—with strikingly different results.

Discussion Starter Questions:

- How do the two main characters in the film view life? How does a person's view of life affect his or her actions?

- What different views concerning morality are offered in this film? Do they reflect our culture's views on the subject? Why or why not?

- Is it ever possible to really escape from our problems? Do you think Judah was able to escape? Why or why not?

- Is justice something we should expect in this life? How should we respond to injustice in the world?

- Do you think moral values are objective or subjective? Why?

- What are the major moral dilemmas that people face today? How should we respond to them?

Movie 9: *Nacho Libre* (2006)

Genre: Comedy

Length: 100 minutes

Rating: PG for some rough action and crude humor including dialogue

Plot: Humble monk and cook Ignacio dreams of the recognition and fame heaped upon the *luchadors*—the masked wrestlers of Mexico—much to the disdain of the priests in the monastery.

Fueled by his passion for wrestling, Ignacio dons a mask and cape and takes the name of Nacho. He enters a local *Lucha Libre* tournament to compete for the $200 prize—so he can buy better food for the kids and achieve the respect he craves. When a new nun, Sister Encarnación, arrives at the monastery, he tries to win her adoration as well as prove that being a *luchador* isn't a sin.

Discussion Starter Questions:

- What is the worst use of fame and fortune you've ever witnessed? What's the best one you've ever seen?

- How did Nacho's hero Ramses disappoint him? Has one of your heroes ever let you down? Explain.

- What qualities do you look for in a hero? What makes a hero's failure so painful? Does this mean we shouldn't have heroes? Explain.

- Was Nacho wrong to want recognition? Explain. Can you relate to his feelings of underappreciation? Why or why not?

- Can someone want more for his or her life and still be content? If so, what does that look like?

- In what areas of your life could you be more content than you currently are? How can you find that contentment?

Movie 10: *Big Fish* (2003)

Genre: Drama/Fantasy

Length: 125 minutes

Rating: Rated PG-13 for a fight scene, some brief images of nudity, and a suggestive reference

Plot: Edward Bloom is dying of cancer, and his son William comes to visit him to say goodbye. The two become tangled in their usual pattern of conflict and misunderstanding. William thinks his father is a lying, dreaming fool. All his life he has heard his father speak in tall tales about his adventures as a young man. Even though Edward's incessant telling of these fantastic stories embarrasses his son, Edward refuses to change his ways. In fact, in the face of William's frustration and annoyance, Edward becomes more adamant about his stories.

Eventually, William begins to sort out the details of his father's past. And perhaps more importantly, he learns some of the reasons why his father spoke so often in mythological terms.

Discussion Starter Questions:

- Which character did you find yourself sympathizing most with in the movie? Why?

- Why do you think Edward insisted on telling his stories in the way that he did? Do you agree or disagree with him?

- What do you think finally changed William's mind about his father?

- What is it about stories that are so important? What role should stories play in our lives? How should our stories be told?

- What are the most important parts of your own life story? How have these moments shaped you? What other ways might you be able to tell that story?

Movie 11: *The Village* (2004)

Genre: Drama/Thriller

Length: 108 minutes

Rating: Rated PG-13 for a scene of violence and frightening situations

Plot: In a small, isolated village, the village's citizens live in constant fear of the woods. Creatures reside there, and they are *not* to be bothered. Likewise, the monsters are not supposed to bother the townspeople. When dead animals start appearing around the village, tension between the people and their mysterious forest-dwelling neighbors mounts, and the villagers grow increasingly fearful.

When an emergency arises in the village, the leaders are faced with a dilemma. After much reluctance, they decide it is best to send out a blind member of their community to journey through the woods to seek help.

Discussion Starter Questions:

• In what ways did the leaders of the village choose the life that they led? What things couldn't they control?

• What's appealing about some of the decisions they made? Would you have made the same decisions? Why or why not?

• Why do people tend to isolate themselves from others with whom they disagree or whom they fear? What are some benefits of isolation? What are some drawbacks?

• What are the responsibilities of the members in a community? How is community practiced in your culture?

• What particular issue did this film force you to confront in your life or in the way you view society?

Movie 12: *Whale Rider* (2002)

Genre: Drama

Length: 101 minutes

Rating: PG-13 for mild language and a drug reference

Plot: A New Zealand tribe, the Whangara, is floundering for lack of a leader. Their mythical history points them back to an original chief, Paikea, who rode the back of a whale to overcome defeat and death. To the present day, the tribal chiefs are believed to be descendants of this single heroic leader. But now, there is no male heir to fill the vacuum of leadership.

Koro searches and trains the available young boys, looking beyond his granddaughter Pai, to fill the void and lead the tribe back to its former glory. While the boys continually disappoint Koro as potential leaders, Pai begins to demonstrate the true signs of being Paikea's heir.

Discussion Starter Questions:

- What role does tradition play in this film? How does this enable or hinder this New Zealand community?

- How should we approach tradition in our own lives?

- How is the ideal Whangara leader portrayed? What are the characteristics of this figure?

- What should we value or be aware of in leadership?

- How is Pai a "messianic" figure in this film? How does she "save" her people? What connections do you see between this film and the story of Jesus?

Movie 13: *Finding Nemo* (2003)

Genre: Animation/Comedy/Family

Length: 100 minutes

Rating: G

Plot: *Finding Nemo* is the story of Marlin, a father clownfish searching for his lost son, Nemo, who has been netted by a diver and taken away in a boat. Along his journey, the normally timid and protective Marlin encounters many dangerous situations, is befriended by a memory-challenged angelfish, and receives help from other sympathetic sea creatures.

Meanwhile Nemo—now in a dentist's fish tank overlooking Sydney Harbor—conspires with his tank mates to escape from the tank before he becomes the dentist's niece's new pet.

Discussion Starter Questions:

- Have you ever tried to make a new habit or change a part of your personality completely on your own? Were you successful? Why or why not?

- How did various sea creatures help Marlin along the way? What can we learn from each of them?

- Does disobedience always have consequences? Why or why not? Is disobedience destructive even if you escape any consequences? Explain.

- What things come to mind when you hear about "God's love for people"? How do you think Marlin's love for Nemo compares to that?

- Do you feel that God loves you personally? Why or why not? If so, how have you seen God express his love to you personally?

Movie 14: *Patch Adams* (1998)

Genre: Comedy/Drama

Length: 115 minutes

Rating: Rated PG-13 for some strong language and crude humor

Plot: This movie, based on a true story, follows the adult life of Hunter "Patch" Adams. Nearing middle age, Hunter realizes how messed up his life is and commits himself to a mental institution. While there, he discovers that helping other patients gives him a joy and fulfillment he's never known. He decides to become a doctor and spend his life helping others.

As Patch pursues his medical degree, he runs into opposition as his ideas about healing don't coincide with those of the medical establishment. After being chastised many times for breaking the rules, Patch opens his own clinic and runs into different kinds of problems in trying to help people.

Discussion Starter Questions:

- In what ways did Patch Adams break the rules in this movie?

- What was good about Patch's approach to medicine? What was bad about his approach?

- Are there times when it's okay to break the rules? If so, when?

- Jesus was criticized by the religious establishment of his day for breaking their rules. (Matthew 12:1-14 is just one example, if you'd like to look.) How was Patch's situation similar to that of Jesus? How was it different?

- What does this movie teach us about the consequences we sometimes face for breaking rules?

Movie 15: *Secondhand Lions* (2003)

Genre: Adventure/Comedy/Drama

Length: 109 minutes

Rating: PG for thematic material, language, and action violence

Plot: As a young teenager, Walter is dumped by his irresponsible mother into the custody of his two uncles, Hub and Garth. Rumor has it they have millions stashed at their Texas ranch, and Walter's mother wants him to find it and gain their favor while she is away for the summer.

While Walter adjusts to living with the two curmudgeons, he discovers there is a lot more to these old men than anyone really knows. Their tales of travel, war, heroism, and love open a new world to Walter. And their companionship enriches Walter's life with surprises and wonder he never knew before.

Discussion Starter Questions:

- Garth and Hub share their stories with Walter. What do they teach Walter through their storytelling?

- Are the stories of Walter's uncles any different than the lies of his mother? Explain.

- Are their stories beneficial? What if they aren't true? Can those kinds of stories still be beneficial? Explain.

- Hub tells Walter it doesn't matter if what he believes in isn't true, as long as what he believes in is worth believing in. Do you agree with that? Why or why not?

Movie 16: *The Incredibles* (2004)

Genre: Animation/Adventure/Family

Length: 115 minutes

Rating: PG for action violence

Plot: Superhero Mr. Incredible is forced into hiding by a surge of lawsuits against superheroes. As a result, he and his superhero wife, Elastigirl, are living out "normal" lives as Bob and Helen Parr. However, Bob longs for the days when superheroes could freely use their powers to rescue people in danger.

When a major crisis arises, Bob can't help himself. He has to stand up against the evil that is threatening the world. In the process, he draws in Elastigirl and their three children, Dash, Violet, and Jack-Jack—who also are found to have superpowers.

Discussion Starter Questions:

- Why was it difficult for Bob to stand up and be Mr. Incredible so he could fight evil in the world? What things were going on in Bob's family that made his situation even more difficult?

- What made Bob decide to stand up and do what was right?

- What good things happened when Bob took action?

- What "superpowers" do you downplay in your own life in order to fit in?

- Why is it sometimes hard for us to stand up and do what's right?

- What—or who—can help us to do the right thing when we're faced with difficult choices?

Movie 17: *Ray* (2004)

Genre: Biography/Drama

Length: 152 minutes

Rating: PG-13 for depiction of drug addiction, sexuality, and some thematic elements

Plot: The movie follows the biography of legendary musician Ray Charles. Born in poverty, Ray became blind at the age of 7, but neither blindness nor poverty stops him. Breaking down racial, musical, and business barriers became his daily routine.

Nonetheless, as Ray's success grew, so did his problems. His appetites for womanizing and heroin threatened to cut his genius and career short. Yet his career would go on to revolutionize the music industry and engage the civil-rights movement.

Discussion Starter Questions:

- Why do people often feel uncomfortable around those with disabilities? How do you think disabled people feel about this?

- What did Ray do to overcome his disability? Do you think you could have done that if you were in his situation? Why or why not?

- What kinds of excuses do people give for not being able to pursue their dreams? How are these excuses like disabilities?

- What does this movie say about achieving one's dreams? How can we help others with disabilities—whether those disabilities are physical, emotional, or spiritual—reach for their dreams?

- What do you need to do personally to achieve your own dreams?

Movie 18: *Unbreakable* (2000)

Genre: Drama

Length: 106 minutes

Rating: PG-13 for mature thematic elements including some disturbing violent content and a crude sexual reference

Plot: When David Dunn emerges as the sole survivor of a tragic train wreck, the wheels are set in motion. A disabled comic-book art gallery owner, Elijah Price, begins to ask him questions about his health and eventually offers David a crazy explanation: David is a real-life superhero.

Slowly, David realizes that in fact his bones do not break, he has never been sick, and he has the power to see evil in the lives of others through physical contact. Once David understands his powers, Elijah prompts him to go out and help people. When David later goes to thank Elijah, he learns the horrible truth about the man who helped him discover his powers.

Discussion Starter Questions:

- What are the most dominant themes of this movie? What is the movie communicating about these ideas?

- What does the film (especially the last scene) suggest about the nature of evil? Do you agree with it? Why or why not?

- Do you think there are forces of evil and forces of good in this world? Explain.

- How does your view of evil affect your view of life?

- How does David's self-discovery affect how he views his life?

- How do David's relationships with his family change during the course of this film? Why? Is it a good thing or a bad one?

Movie 19: *Glory Road* (2006)

Genre: Drama/Sport

Length: 106 minutes

Rating: PG for racial issues including violence and epithets, and momentary language

Plot: This movie is based on a true story. Don Haskins, a girls' basketball coach, is hired to become the men's basketball coach of the Texas Western Miners. He goes on the recruiting trail to find the best talent in the land, black *or* white—in the mid-'60s, when black and white were seldom mixed anywhere, let alone on a college basketball court.

The team Haskins puts together—of seven black players and five white—is repeatedly ridiculed and threatened as they travel around the country. And yet, Haskins and his Miners come together as a team and reach the NCAA championship game against perennial powerhouse Kentucky.

Discussion Starter Questions:

- What risks did Haskins and his coaches take in recruiting black players at that time? What risks did the players themselves—both black *and* white—take in accepting Haskins' offer?

- Besides their accomplishments as a team, what other advances did you see both on the court and off because of the team Haskins put together?

- Why was it difficult for the coaches and players to listen and learn from each other? What can you learn from this?

- What kind of people do you struggle most with seeing as equals? How would seeing them through God's eyes change your relationships?

- What kinds of risks might you be called to take right now? What do you think your first step is in accepting that challenge?

Movie 20: *The Truman Show* (1998)

Genre: Drama/Sci-Fi

Length: 103 minutes

Rating: PG for thematic elements and mild language

Plot: Truman Burbank thinks he lives an ordinary life. Too ordinary. He wants to get out of his small town, the home he's never left. But as he begins to scheme to get away, obstacles emerge from every side—obstacles too extreme or coincidental to ignore. His wife tries to keep him grounded—and at home—by pointing out all the reasons he should just stay put. His best friend assures Truman that nothing is amiss—that if Truman's paranoid ideas were true, he'd have to be in on them, too.

But Truman won't give up. He maneuvers around those manipulating him, faces his worst fears, and finds himself in a position more difficult than any he had to face in his ordinary existence.

Discussion Starter Questions:

- *The Truman Show* was originally released in 1998. How have some of the (at the time) absurd concepts of this movie since become reality?

- Truman believes his life is authentic (he's the "true-man" in the show). If a person believes something, though it is not accurate, is that good enough?

- What are some myths from the past that people have believed to be true? What do you believe to be a myth that others embrace today with their whole hearts?

- By leaving his staged life, what did Truman lose? What did he gain? Do you think it was worth it? Why or why not?

Simple Service Ideas

SURE, service projects help those people we serve. But serving others has a hidden benefit that many people overlook: It also does something to *us*. God doesn't just mean for service to be a way to right the world's wrongs—he also wants it to shape us to become more Christ-like. Christian service can break our addictions to our own needs, shake us into awareness, and expose us to a kind of love of we might not otherwise be aware of.

You can also think of service as kind of a safe level of evangelism. In other words, be ready if people ask what is motivating you to serve.

The ideas here will help children's, youth, and adult groups alike take the first practical steps toward getting involved in the world outside your church doors. As you take these ideas and prayerfully apply them, expect both your hearts and the hearts of those you serve to be opened further to the love of Jesus.

10 Service Ideas for Children's Groups

Idea 1　It's in the Bag

What better way to find items and gifts that will delight a child than to have another child choose them? And what better way to instill a sense of giving and an understanding of the plight of less fortunate children than by involving children in the process of giving them?

Give your children gallon-sized zipper baggies, and challenge them to fill their baggies with items they believe will bless an underprivileged child. Teach them what "underprivileged" means; provide meaningful examples so children can understand those they will be caring for. Tell a story about a child who lives in an impoverished place, or tell about an orphan without a home or family. Let the children know and realize that many children live without the conveniences they might take for granted, such as a toothbrush or shoes or even one favorite toy. Involve parents by asking them to supervise and finance the shopping and purchasing of the items. Set a dollar limit if desired.

Include items such as small balls or games, crayons or markers, hygiene products, stickers, socks, candy, and hair-care items. Once you have determined whom the baggies will go to, you'll have a better idea of specific items that will benefit them.

Use an instant camera to provide children with photos of themselves to include in their baggies. Also help them write short notes to include with their gifts. Mark the baggies for a recipient of a specific age and/or gender, if appropriate. (You might wish to assign baggies according to age and gender as well.)

Work with established agencies to set up the connection needed to distribute the baggies, whether they are for local residents or children in a distant country. If feasible, allow the children to deliver their baggies themselves—it will add a personal touch for the kids receiving them and add significance for the kids delivering them. Whether your children deliver the baggies or not, obtain follow-up information about the distribution of the baggies so kids can follow up with letters. If the children weren't present for the giving, it will also provide feedback to the children about their child and how their gifts were received.

After the project is completed, ask your kids the following questions:

- What did you like most about caring for other children?

- What was most difficult for you as you put together your gifts and gave them to another?

- What did you learn about the other kids that you didn't know before?

Idea 2   **Pen Pal and Planted Pot**

Here's a great opportunity for youngsters to get to know and care for seniors! Each child will develop a relationship with a senior pen pal by writing a letter, decorating a flower pot and planting a flower, then personally delivering his or her note and flower pot.

First, find a group of senior citizens willing to participate in your project. All you need to ask of them is that they write letters to the kids in your group and allow a visit from your group so their pen pals can present them with some small gifts. (If you're having trouble finding a group of seniors outside your church, you could still try this with a Sunday school class in your church comprised of seniors. It's a great first step in getting kids connected with the elderly in your church!)

Second, assign one senior to each child in your group. Give the seniors their assigned child's name, and ask that they write a note about themselves to the child, specifying when the letter needs to be delivered by. Set the date prior to when the children will meet to decorate their pots and write their own notes. You can have the seniors mail their letters individually, or you can collect and deliver them in person.

In turn, have each child write a note to his or her assigned senior. If you're dealing with an age group too young to write notes, have them color pictures that show themselves doing something they enjoy. Help each child address or label his or her note to the pen pal.

Once the notes are written, have the children decorate flower pots. Use small terra cotta pots, and have the children paint them or glue on decorative items such as buttons and beads. Then fill each pot with dry potting soil, and press some seeds (such as alyssum or baby's breath) into the surface. Print out instructions that say "Water Me and Watch Me Grow" on small slips of paper, and tape them to a toothpick like a small flag. Stick the toothpick flag into the soil of each pot, and you're ready to go.

Arrange a meeting time when the children's group can visit the seniors, and have them deliver their pots and notes. This may also be a good time to let the kids get to know their pen pals better through games or story time, as time and circumstances allow.

Idea 3   Kids Visiting Kids

Kids are kids, no matter what the setting. Contact a local children's home in your area to ask if the members of your children's ministry group could come to visit. Most communities have residential living centers for children with family problems or special needs. If your community doesn't have such a facility, see if a neighboring town does. Or change your focus to children in long-term care in your local hospital.

Explain that you'll bring the games, art supplies, and refreshments—and the kids, of course!

Be aware that some residents of the home may have emotional difficulties. You'll want to work closely with the director of the children's home to make sure you follow guidelines. You'll also want to have signed parental permission slips for your kids, as well as plenty of adult supervision during your outing.

But don't let the possible precautions you might need to face hinder you from making the effort. Many of the residents who live in children's homes are starved for attention and rarely receive visitors, even from family members. Who knows? Some of your kids may just forge lasting friendships that originate from the simple sharing of the love of Jesus.

Idea 4   Be a Sport

Have you ever sat through an extra-inning Little League game, with the hot sun beating down on your head—*and* your cooler is empty? Wouldn't a nice, cold soft drink have been most welcome, especially if it were delivered by a smiling child? And if it were *free*?

This is a service that kids in your church can easily provide in your community, at any time of year. Scout out upcoming children's sporting events in your area—baseball games, swim meets, hockey matches, soccer games, or football contests, to name just a few. Gather whatever kinds of refreshments might be most welcome to spectators at the events—such as cold drinks at a summer soccer match or hot chocolate at a frigid football game. Then hand out the drinks at whatever event you've decided on.

Make sure to have plenty of adult supervision, and never let kids wander off on their own. It would probably be best to get permission before the event so you can station your kids at an entrance. Explain to your kids that the goal is not to "convert" spectators into new members of your church but to provide a warm and welcoming introduction to Jesus' love.

Before this outreach, have T-shirts printed with your church's name and location. Or let kids design their own T-shirts. You might also consider printing small fliers with your church information on them. Again, kids would have fun helping to design these identifying fliers.

Idea 5 **Say It With Flowers**

No matter what the season, few things cheer an atmosphere or attitude more quickly than a lovely flower display. Take the term *love-ly* literally as you help your children's group fill a local nursing home with the love of God.

If you choose to do this outreach in spring or summer, buy a variety of colorful annual flowers. Then have your kids spend a Saturday morning planting the flowers in outdoor beds at the facility. (Get permission first, of course!) After all their hard work, let kids visit indoors with residents and share some cold refreshments you brought along.

If planting the flowers in outdoor beds isn't feasible, let children plant several free-standing pots that residents can enjoy in common areas indoors. And if you choose to complete this outreach in fall or winter, let kids get creative and make their own flowers! Depending on the age of your children, homemade flowers can range from simple construction paper tulips to elaborate craft foam bouquets. Children can still deliver the flowers and enjoy a seasonal treat with residents.

As kids are planting or making their flowers, discuss these questions:

• What did your flowers need in order to grow?

• What does our *faith* need to grow? How is it like what flowers need? How is it different?

• What are some other ways we can reach out and "plant" God's love in other people?

Idea 6   Stock the Shelves

Help your children's group surprise a local food pantry by stocking its shelves. More than just collecting a few cans of food, this could be a kid-directed outreach project from start to finish.

First, contact your intended recipient so you'll have their guidelines and wish list in hand. Second, facilitate a planning meeting with your kids. Note: The key word here is *facilitate*. Don't *tell* kids what they're going to do. Explain the basic scope of the project, then let kids grapple with how to get it done.

Here are some details they'll need to nail down: What's their goal in terms of how much food can be realistically collected? Will they try to collect the food themselves or develop a donation plan? If they ask for donations, whom will they ask? How will they get the word out?

A churchwide food drive is probably the easiest for kids to tackle. If they decide, however, on a neighborhood drive or asking for donations in public, be sure to get parents' permission and participation so you'll have plenty of adult supervision and guidance.

Once they've outlined their approach, let kids do as much of the actual preparation as possible. They could make their own advertisements for the outreach and hang the signs throughout the church. They could speak at church services to create a buzz for their efforts. They could decide where and when to collect the food donations and then sort them by type.

Most importantly, make sure kids get the opportunity to conclude the outreach themselves. Don't just deliver the donations yourself. Set up a time for kids to come with you, and let kids stock the shelves at the recipient's location. Let them meet with the director and volunteers so they can see how the food pantry actually operates. Not only will they have the pleasure of a job completed, but they'll also feel a part of an outreach much bigger than themselves.

Idea 7   Soup's On!

Your kids will get a real taste of servanthood when they volunteer at a local soup kitchen. Arrange details with the facility director as to when and how the children in your group can best serve. Explain that, as much as possible, you want your kids to have a hands-on experience.

Perhaps your kids can come in early and help prepare the food to be offered that day. After a quick course in sanitation practices, they could easily handle such simple tasks as stirring, pouring, and measuring. They might also arrange platters of bread or sandwich ingredients, fill condiment containers, and clean and set the tables.

Kids could also make centerpieces to adorn the tables or make signs to welcome the patrons. If appropriate, let some of your kids greet people as they arrive for the meal. Others in your group could help with the serving and behind-the-scenes continued preparation.

Be sure, too, that everyone helps with the cleanup process. It's important for kids to see how the whole operation works, from start to finish. By doing so, they'll also gain a deeper appreciation for the unsung servants in their towns and neighborhoods.

Idea 8   A Little Relief

There are needy kids all over the world, and *your* kids can help!

Organize a kid-to-kid relief effort to help a children's charity of your choice. Make your project a one-time event or even a quarterly or seasonal outreach. Here are a few ideas to help you get started:

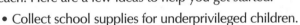

- Collect school supplies for underprivileged children.
- Gather toiletry supplies for kids in impoverished or war-torn countries.
- Collect and wrap new toys to give away at Christmas.
- Buy Bibles for kids who can't afford their own.
- Send teddy bears to hospitalized children.

Whatever avenue of outreach you choose, add a personal element to your project. Let the children in your ministry make and sign cards to accompany your gifts. Take a class snapshot to send along. (Check with your church first to determine if you need parental permission.) If possible, set up an ongoing means of communication between the kids in your ministry and the recipients of your outreach.

Ask recipients to write back to your kids and send pictures of themselves, or set up a special e-mail address at your church so kids can correspond with their counterparts. The more your kids can get to know the needs and hearts of other children around the nation or world, the more they'll realize the need to spread the love of Jesus far and near.

If your church uses The Easy VBS® program from Group Publishing, your kids will already be familiar with its Operation Kid-to-Kid™ outreach. You can build from that experience to make your project a quarterly or seasonal outreach event. If your church isn't familiar with Operation Kid-to-Kid and you'd like to know more, check it out at www.ok2k.org.

Idea 9   Military Ministry

Support our troops as you build a powerful prayer partnership between the kids in your ministry and those men and women serving in our nation's military.

Your outreach program could take on a variety of forms. Kids could write letters or make greeting cards to send to soldiers, especially those serving in combat zones overseas. Stress that kids should mention that your group is praying for the soldiers and asking God's protection for their safety, and be sure to build a prayer time into your weekly meetings. In addition, encourage kids to pray for soldiers every day on their own. Emphasize that prayer is a powerful tool God has put at our disposal.

Kids could also make simple crafts with Bible verses on them to send to the soldiers. For example, a child might write a favorite Bible verse on a small wooden craft heart. Or kids might make bead bracelets spelling out a Scripture reference.

There have been recent news articles stating that many soldiers always carry small, meaningful items with them into combat. The crafts your kids make might just become those items!

Idea 10   Cancer Care

Cancer patients often report feeling isolated during their illness. People don't seem to know what to say, so they sometimes avoid contact altogether. Let your children's group address this problem by reaching out to people battling cancer.

Let your kids decide the scope of the outreach project. Giving children a say in the decision will not only foster feelings of ownership but will help develop critical-thinking skills in heads and hearts that are just beginning to take on servant qualities. Allowing children to settle on their own project scope is a first step in teaching kids how to set realistic goals and how to work as a unit.

Kids might elect to create cards of encouragement for cancer patients. If so, provide a variety of art supplies for kids to share, such as colored paper, construction paper, poster board, gel pens, paint, sponges, specialty scissors, small paint brushes, stickers, fine-tipped neon markers, glitter glue, stampers, and ink pads. You might also provide small accents to glue on the cards, such as buttons and ribbon.

Children might also want to create simple crafts to cheer up patients. Stuffed bears could be a symbol of comfort, or cheerful pictures could add color to hospital rooms or homes.

Whatever kids decide, have Bibles handy so children can include favorite verses of encouragement, strength, and hope. Remind kids that one of the most effective ways they can let cancer patients know that they care is to pray for them. Make sure that praying for the patients is an essential element of whatever project kids decide on.

Let kids accompany you when you deliver the cards or crafts of encouragement. Then in the following weeks, remind kids to follow through and pray!

9 Service Ideas for Youth Groups

Idea 1   Cancel Youth Group?

Yes, cancel youth group. Youth group is a fantastic creation of the 20th century, but a change of pace and opening up an opportunity to serve will be well worth the sacrifice. Cancel youth group, and instead partner with a local service organization where your students can participate on a regular basis, during your regular youth group time. This way, busy students already have the time available and are not stressed trying to add another event to their schedule.

If your ministry has Bible studies or Sunday school at a different time, continue meeting with those so that your students are continually in an environment to be spiritually fed. If your ministry only meets one night a week, consider having a dinner together beforehand where you can pray for each other, study Scripture, and worship together before serving together.

Investigate local organizations, faith-based or not, where your students can help. One idea is sorting food at a homeless shelter. It might seem like a boring, thankless job, but your students could make it fun as they work hard together. They could also volunteer in a tutoring program. High school students can easily be partnered with younger children learning to read or learning basic math. A third idea is a nursing home. Many elderly folks appreciate all kinds of visitors, and having this as a regularly scheduled event will build a community of familiar faces.

Pick a local organization that does not necessarily know what it means to receive God's love, and watch your students interact in ways that bring others to know Jesus. Be sure to debrief after each visit, so your youth group members will gain a deeper understanding of the service they've done and where God may want to lead them next.

Idea 2   Serving Single Parents

Twice as many dishes to wash, twice as many rides to school, twice as many shoes to tie, twice as many hugs to give—but only half the energy, half the time, and half the people. Single parents work, and work hard, without always having another adult to talk to or a backup when they need a minute to breathe.

Give these probably tired people a helping hand by making some of the everyday things a little easier. Provide once-a-month babysitting for single parents. If it's on a weeknight, right after school, or on a Saturday morning, it'll give your parents the opportunity to schedule things like doctor's appointments, runs to the grocery store, or just a little downtime.

Consider also offering a monthly or bimonthly night out for these parents, and have all the kids in your care play together during that time. Parents can enjoy a night to themselves, dinner with a friend, a non-cartoon movie, and simply the peace of knowing that their children are being cared for by the students at your church, playing with other children in a safe environment. The children will look forward to the opportunity to play and see their friends, and it only will take a few students (depending on the size of your group) a few hours to serve in this way.

Check with local rules and church policies for running this kind of child care, even if it's informal. You are probably required to meet certain adult/child ratios. Church Volunteer Central (www.churchvolunteercentral.com) is one great site to obtain more information on guidelines, as well as other volunteer ideas. Make sure to have adult volunteers present as well, working alongside the students who are playing with the children. A local business might even be willing to provide healthy snacks. Encourage your students to meet together to plan some fun activities. Children's ministry volunteers would be a great resource for games and other activities.

Depending on your church's facility and resources, consider advertising around the area. There might be some exhausted single parents who are drawn to your church and eventually a relationship with Jesus by being served in this way.

Idea 3   After-School Care

It has been said that the most dangerous hours in the week for students are from 3:00 to 5:00 p.m.—the hours immediately after school and before parents arrive home. It has also been argued that kids in middle school and junior high need more supervision than 8-year-olds. Kids of these ages are old enough to have dangerous influences but not old enough to truly process the long-term consequences of their actions.

Make your church a student-friendly environment after school, and if possible, provide transportation from the local middle school or junior high. Students love to hang out—even if it's while doing nothing or doing homework—so no plans are necessarily needed. All they need is a place. If your church is not a good location, see if a church member would be willing to open his or her home. You might also consider talking to a local community center or recreation building to see if they'd allow you to use their space.

If your church does not have a youth pastor or staff member who could be around during this time or the space to host this, talk to youth volunteers and parents who are around during these hours and see who could help. These adults will form lasting relationships with the students that neither will forget.

Contact a few local businesses and see if they'd be willing to donate snacks. Movie theaters might donate matinee tickets once a month, and places like ice-skating arenas might be willing to offer free passes or discounts. A once-a-month field trip would be a blast for students and volunteers alike!

Idea 4   Here to There

Students often have a tough journey transitioning from grade school to middle school or from middle school to high school. Strategically plan some "here-to-there" events that focus on building community for the incoming class. Make it your goal to connect with each student who's participating—and to connect students with one another.

Have older students serve and lead these events, and challenge them to demonstrate their maturity (and coolness!) by hanging out with the younger teenagers.

Examples of here-to-there events include a guys' or girls' night out, weekend camping trip, scavenger hunt, big welcome party, and dedication and commitment service.

After your event, ask your students:

- What memory do you think you'll carry longest from this event?

- Why is it important to mark big transitions in life? What's the next event in your life that you think should be celebrated as a milestone?

- What's a transition in life that isn't celebrated but you think should be?

- How can this kind of experience bring us closer as a group?

Idea 5   Do-It-Yourself Day Camp

Children in lower-income areas are sometimes left alone to play during summer days. Parents are off at work, and there probably isn't the money to send them to day camp or other programs in the area. Work with a community center in an area that has the dream and perhaps already the beginnings of a program like this. Your students can volunteer, plan, and facilitate a camp for children who may never get to experience something like this.

Find a location where parents won't have to drive their children, if you can. Pick a park that has a shelter, in case of rain, and work with the community center or sponsoring organization to make sure your students are following child-care laws and other guidelines.

Divide the day into games, snacks, and crafts, and if possible, depending on the organization, have a short Bible lesson to talk about how much Jesus loves these children. You might even consider putting together a VBS program for those days. Parents might not mind that their children are receiving Christian teaching because they are being taken care of so well and having fun. It might be the only opportunity some of these kids have to hear about Jesus.

Donating a few mornings a week for a summer will have a dramatic impact on the kids, their parents, and the organization with which you're working.

Idea 6   Getting Gorgeous

Even the biggest tomboys, deep down inside, imagine getting into a beautiful gown and being the belle of the ball. Prom is one of those opportunities. It's a chance for the girls who never or rarely dress up to put on a gorgeous gown and shine. However, events like this are expensive.

Contact a nearby high school that is in a lower-income area or an organization that deals with clothing donations, and offer to give them dresses for girls to go to school social functions. Then have your students organize a

Prom Dress Drive at their school. Many girls buy formal dresses like this and only wear them once or twice. Contact college alumni of your ministry, and ask if they have any dresses from high school that they never wear anymore. Make sure to have them cleaned before donating them.

This might sound like a girl-only event, and it might be for your ministry. However, remind your guys that working with this project does not mean that they have to donate a dress. Phone calls, transporting the dresses, and promoting the idea are all parts of this project.

To a high school girl who wants so badly to participate in a school function—especially if she feels like the only one who can't go to an event—this will take away the stress of feeling left out. It will give her a sense of belonging, allow her the privilege to feel beautiful and special, and create lifelong memories.

Idea 7   Let It Snow!

Some of your students might be praying for feet of snow, hoping that it will cancel school. Their dream, however, can be a nightmare for others. For those who struggle to shovel their own walks and driveways, snow may trap them in their homes, cause much stress, be an expensive mess, and lead to potential injury.

Rally your troops and form a team that's willing to be on call during snowstorms to shovel, whether school is canceled or not. Figure out what students live in what neighborhoods, and then advertise in those areas. Try to keep the "shovelers" and the "shovelees" within walking distance of each other so students can do this easily and safely before school, if the roads are bad.

You'll need an adult who is willing to coordinate the efforts and make the decisions about whether or not to send out the troops. A phone chain might work well for this. Have the adult call one student, who gets the message and calls the next student, and so on. Using parents as contacts might be wise as well, considering how hard it is to wake up some students extra-early.

If possible, also consider sending an adult volunteer around to the different locations to deliver hot chocolate, if the roads are safe. It would be a much appreciated treat!

Idea 8   Neighborhood Bicycle Exchange

Children grow. Bicycles don't. It's that simple. Seats and handlebars can only be raised so high. And sometimes children grow quite fast, leaving a bike in fantastic condition with no one to ride it.

Have parents bring in used bicycles that their children have outgrown, do whatever work might be needed on them, and give them to a local shelter or organization that provides toys for families who can't afford such things.

You'll need volunteers to coordinate advertising the project with specific deadlines. This could be done by fliers at the grocery stores in town, blurbs in the local newspaper, and announcements in the church bulletin. You'll also need volunteers who can physically store and clean up the bicycles. Talk to a sports store or bike shop to see if they'd be willing to donate some grease or a bike chain, and possibly even a few hours' labor for free.

Next, pick out a time and place to give the bikes away. You could use your church or a local business so that it is less intimidating to community members who do not have a relationship with any church. Have information about other ministries available.

Idea 9   Compassion International—and Local

You've seen the commercials, and your students probably have, too. The young faces from third-world countries, the faces of hunger, the faces of hopelessness…the faces that you want to help but don't know how. "Adopting" a child might be a stretch for students; a dollar a day could literally break the bank for them. That doesn't mean they don't want to help.

Work with your youth group to coordinate adopting a child together. (See www.compassion.com for more information.) This is one way that your youth group can reach out and love others around the world, one person at a time. Have them take turns writing letters to the children.

Also, instead of having your students ask their parents for cash, encourage them to come up with ways to earn it themselves. They could baby-sit, tutor, mow lawns, or do a variety of other odd jobs. Students can take the opportunity to share with their "employers" that they are doing this for a Compassion child, and that might open up the opportunity to share about God's love and your church.

Make sure that your students understand that this is a significant commitment. It's not something that they can do for a summer because it sounds fun, then drop once the school year gets too busy. When students graduate, give them the chance to keep their Compassion child, but at that point, they need to oversee and coordinate letters and money themselves.

If you have a small group fizzle out or graduate, pass the child on to a new, younger group of students. After even only one year of doing this, your entering students will hear of and look forward to this being a part of their experience in your ministry. Anticipating this kind of ownership in the ministry will also help make the transition from the children's or junior high program easier.

21 Service Ideas for Adult Groups of All Kinds

Idea 1　Community Breakfast

Your church can join with other churches in the community to offer a free breakfast that's open to the entire community. It can become a regular event that draws people from around the area, from all walks of life.

Here's one way to approach it: Your men's ministry can meet with the pastor to find out what churches he or she would suggest calling to take part in this outreach. A volunteer will call other churches to find a contact person to work with. Decide how many churches you want to participate and how many you need before you plan the first breakfast. The churches can rotate hosting the event.

The women's ministry could take care of getting the word out in your community—for example, in newspapers, in public service announcements, or on radio stations. Highlight that this is a free event for anyone who wants to come and an opportunity to meet and visit their neighbors. The women's ministry can also take care of the kitchen chores and cooking—unless one or two of the men specialize in cooking pancakes or other breakfast foods.

The men's and youth ministries can set up and clean up the dining hall. The youth can also help in serving guests.

Be sure to make this a *full* breakfast. Instead of just rolls or cereal, include meat, fruit, and eggs. You may want to accept donations to help offset the cost of the food. However, make it clear that no one has to donate. Open and end the breakfast with prayer. One of the churches can provide a short devotion.

This outreach offers an opportunity for people in your community to get to know each other, and it can bring unity among the churches in the community. It can be done on a monthly or quarterly basis, depending on the number of churches involved.

Idea 2   Oh, Baby!

Unwed mothers need support. Your ministry could help one (or more) of these women by providing a baby dresser filled with clothes, a playpen, a rocker, and other things babies (and moms) need. Contact a local pregnancy resource center about your proposed project, and obtain a list of suggested items. Ask the center what its policy is regarding contact with the unwed moms. Some wish to remain anonymous; however, others might be open to delivery of the gifts by two or three of your volunteers.

Advertise this project in your church's bulletin and announcements. Provide the list of items, and dedicate two or three Sundays to collecting the items. Also, suggest that the givers include notes or cards of encouragement, left unsealed for the local pregnancy center to read and determine their inclusion. Your ministry would buy the dresser, playpen, or rocker and place it in the church lobby. Volunteers can check off the items as people bring them. Be sure to also take time to pray with your givers for the mom and her unborn baby.

Make arrangements to deliver the completed project, cards, and notes to the pregnancy center or to the mom. If the woman is willing to see some ladies from your ministry, they can visit with her for a short while and offer to pray for her and her baby. Ask if she has any specific prayer requests. Be gentle and kind.

This is an outreach that can be done as often as you like, as local pregnancy centers always know of unwed mothers.

Idea 3   Movin' On Up...

One thing we can count on in today's society is its transience. Families are always moving—whether it's a transfer or an "upward" (or "downward" move) in the same area. Young adults are also constantly on the move—to and from college, to new apartments, or as they prepare to get married and start a new life together. It's a stressful time, no matter what the reason. Your group can be there to reduce some of the stress—as well as some of the physical load.

Identify a family or families facing an upcoming move—word of mouth between those in your church and their friends and neighbors is usually enough. Let the person who finds out about the need approach his or her friend or neighbor and ask whether it'd be OK for members of the church to come over and help him or her move. Usually, that person will welcome it with open arms—and start putting the boxes into *your* open arms.

What do you need to make this a success? Volunteers! Many moves can be completed within a few hours if there are enough people helping. Find a system that works for your ministry: e-mail, word of mouth, sign-up sheets, or another idea. Let volunteers know the needs for each particular move, as well as dates and times. At a minimum, find out the following:

- Does the person need help packing the week before?
- Is the mover renting a van or looking for volunteers with trucks or trailers?
- Will he or she be ready to load the van on Friday night, or does everything need to happen on a Saturday morning (or some other time)?

If you can pull together enough volunteers, it's possible (if it's a local move) to load the van, drive it to the new location, and unload it by lunchtime. Those who aren't loading and unloading can be cleaning and helping the "loaders" to stay hydrated. You could even buy the pizza afterward, instead of expecting the people you're moving to feed you (after all, they're *moving*—money is usually very much in flux during this time, and it'd be one less thing for them to think about). Either way, having lunch together is a nice reward and a time to relax and talk a bit after all that hard work.

Idea 4   Senior Cleanup Crew

Picture a group of senior adults scraping and painting a house for a needy family, rebuilding a porch, developing a section in a local park, or cleaning up a messy spot in the neighborhood. Of course you must get permission on these projects, but the powers-that-be will likely jump at the opportunity to have volunteers help clean up and fix up.

Within a few miles of nearly every church in America there are houses, streets, parks, schools, or streets needing some cleanup. Take some time and drive to an area where you see needs—buildings that need painting, broken fences, or trash in a park or along a street.

Go to the proper authorities to ask if they're willing to accept some volunteer help. Most officials will, but if not, look for other projects in other nearby communities.

Then figure out a way to present the need to your senior adult ministry. This could be as simple as taking some photos of areas, preparing a slide presentation, or trying something a bit more sophisticated like a PowerPoint or

DVD presentation. Try not to give away that these pictures were taken within five miles of your church. After the presentation, ask your group where they think the pictures were taken. Then lead a discussion on needs "outside of our walls." Ask if there are any in the group who would be willing to become part of a one-time "our own backyard" ministry. Select a project that can be accomplished in four to five workdays.

You could even make it an annual event for your seniors' group—or better yet, include older youth and young adults, and make it an intergenerational project. Give lots of positive recognition to everyone involved. Have a dedication service prior to the project, write up an article for your church newsletter and the local newspaper, and share the results with the larger church family after the project is complete.

You could also check with your town's social-service agencies to get names of families who are worthy of a good service ministry and let others know your church is being a good neighbor. If you decide to do a project with individuals, you'll of course need to speak privately with them before any announcements are made or publicity is done.

Idea 5   God's Sweethearts

Valentine's Day can be an emotional downer for single women. Your ministry can bless them by providing a special brunch or dinner on Valentine's Day Saturday (or the Saturday before Valentine's Day).

Send out invitations to women both inside and outside your church. Let them know that you will provide babysitting for whatever age groups you can accommodate. Ask for an RSVP, but also ask one or two volunteers to follow up with phone calls or e-mails a week or so after invitations go out.

Or take it a step further: Have another team of volunteers contact people in each lady's life—children, friends, or co-workers—and ask them to express what that woman means to them. Then at the brunch, present to each attendee these sentiments written on lovely paper or cards.

Make the brunch special with china, glassware, and silverware instead of plastic or paper. Play instrumental music softly in the background. Use flowers for centerpieces, and give each lady a rose and a box of candy—or a special book or journal.

Invite a speaker, perhaps your pastor, to talk about God's love and how special each lady is to him. Most importantly, allow ladies being served time to interact with the women in your ministry and other attendees. Be sure that your volunteers spread themselves out among the tables. This is a day to serve these single ladies with the love and grace of Jesus. Your outreach can produce lasting results in their lives.

Idea 6   Mother's Day Dinner

Men are good at many things, but remembering holidays…well, let's just say that sometimes a reminder can be quite helpful. Your small group can help make that reminder into a special night for everyone involved.

Have the men in your small group plan a Mother's Day dinner for the special women in their lives. (If one of the spouses doesn't normally come to your group, this is a great opportunity to get him or her involved as well.) You could also turn this into a multigenerational celebration—get the kids involved with helping; invite the grandmothers and honor them as well. You could also consider inviting neighbors who don't come to your group to take part in the fun.

But make sure the dads are in charge. This is an opportunity for them to use their creative abilities without blowing their masculine cover, and it will allow those with the gift of administration to use it somewhere other than work, a house project, or the church budget. Let one or more of your men pull the plan together and get everything assigned. There's probably at least one cook among your men—let him have at it. And buy flowers—c'mon guys, it's Mother's Day.

Throw in some games, too. One fun idea would be to take turns blindfolding Mom, letting everyone shout at once, and having her try to find her "child" amidst the din (even if it's the child she married!).

If one of your men is particularly gifted with video software, let him create a video or slideshow of the wives and mothers you're honoring tonight. It could be a very powerful time watching it together at the end of your evening.

Idea 7   Summertime Joys

Many organizations provide kids' camps for homeless or underprivileged kids in the summer. Your church can bless those workers and children for a few days. Contact an organization that conducts one of these camps in your area, and ask about opportunities to serve.

Men's, women's, and youth ministries can provide volunteers for a week. They may be needed as counselors, lifeguards, cooks, or craft teachers. That team will train and participate in the camp for the whole week. Your team can also find out if they can provide any supplies or equipment to help stretch the camp's funds.

Usually workers have to clean up after the children leave. A second team of volunteers can go in fresh to help with this. Workers will be tired physically and mentally, and it will bless them to go home a little earlier after they send off the last campers. They can look forward to a shower and a nap instead of one more day of dirty cabins, bathrooms, and campgrounds.

As time goes on, your church may feel comfortable taking charge of a week of camp. That would entail providing leadership, training, and staff for that week. This will depend on your relationship with the workers at the camp and the dedication of your volunteers.

This one week of camp may be the only time that an inner-city child gets away from a difficult environment. You can show him or her that someone cares, and you can show him or her the love of Jesus. Your church can make a difference in children's lives by spending just one week with them at camp.

Idea 8   **Backpacks for the Homeless**

Children in a homeless shelter need school supplies and backpacks when school begins. Volunteers from your men's and women's ministries can bless these children and their parents by providing for these needs. This outreach will also help the shelter by easing its burden of getting the children ready for school.

Contact a local shelter in early summer to discuss the idea. Find out the number of children in each grade level at the time. (This number could change, so call a week prior to your outreach to confirm numbers and grade levels.) Set a date, time, and place for the event, and ask how many volunteers should come. Tell the staff that you would also like some of their volunteers or workers to join you. They'll know the residents and the best ways to serve them.

The women's ministry can obtain supply lists for each grade from the school district by calling or going to its Web site. Then it can set up a collection point for the items and funds needed for a two- or three-week period. Station at least two volunteers at that point. One will check off the items; the other will collect and keep track of money. Start receiving the items and money in late July or early August (depending on when the school year starts), or as soon as ads for sales on school supplies appear.

Volunteers from the men's and women's ministries can sort the supplies and provide any items or backpacks that are missing. The men's ministry can pack the supplies into backpacks, deliver them to the shelter, and set up the distribution room.

Both ministries can join shelter workers to pray with parents and give out the backpacks. Ask if the parents have specific requests for prayer, or share the gospel with them if the opportunity presents itself. This ministry can help your church develop a relationship with the shelter for future events.

Idea 9   Christmas Toy Shop

Urban churches serve people who often have great needs. The church is there day in and day out, ministering to the community. Suburban churches often want to help in urban areas but don't know how. Have a suburban and an urban church come together for a Christmas toy giveaway at the urban church.

Set a date and time, then have volunteers from each church meet to plan the giveaway and pray for parents who come to shop for their children. This part of the event should be open only to parents so children won't know what they are getting for Christmas.

Both churches collect toys. The suburban church may well bring more toys, and that's OK. Each church's men's ministry packs and takes toys to the designated place for the "toy store." Men and women from both churches set up the store and a check-in table. Volunteers from each church help parents sign in their names and children's names and ages. Other volunteers escort them to the various areas for baby toys, little girls' toys, older boys' toys, and so on. After parents finish shopping, a volunteer from one of the churches can offer to pray with them.

This outreach can link the two churches for service in the name of Jesus. Parents' needs are met, and volunteers are blessed in their serving. It's also an opportunity for the two churches to develop a relationship that they can pursue further over time.

Idea 10   Senior Story Source

Children love stories. And seniors are a great source for stories like no other! Build the connection between generations by facilitating a story time between kids and those who've been around the block a few more times.

Arrange regular meeting times for seniors to spend time with children, either one-on-one or with several youngsters, to read and tell stories. Monthly or weekly gathering times, with a different storyteller each time, will allow the children opportunity to hear from a wide variety of storytellers.

Ask your seniors to start by reading aloud a select story on a subject that corresponds with additional real-life stories they share with the group—then follow up with their own stories. For example, the storyteller might read *Mike Mulligan and His Steam Shovel,* then relate his own experiences working as a construction worker 50 years ago and what life was like during that time.

A question-and-answer time after the stories are told is a good way for children to explore ideas and learn more about others, their lives, and other times.

There are many resources available from the library, bookstore, national organizations, and online to help teach about the process of storytelling. Connect your storytellers with any support they may need or find helpful.

Idea 11   Crisis-Pregnancy Baby Shower

Help the young women in your community who are coping with crisis pregnancies. Contact your local crisis-pregnancy center to find out what supplies the center needs. Then host a baby shower to provide the center with all those items.

Invite all the women in your church to come. Make a list of supplies available ahead of time, and encourage women to purchase the items and bring them to the baby shower. Have the women bring their purchased items to the shower and put them on display tables.

Use baby shower decorations for your party. At the shower, give women time to view all of the donated items. Then enjoy baby shower food—serve a decorated cake, punch, mints, and nuts. Invite a woman from the crisis-pregnancy center to give a presentation about the young women who are served by the organization. Then break up into small groups of three or four to pray specifically for the center, the pregnant women, and the babies they will have.

Some women may want to do more. Encourage them to volunteer at the center. Women could even volunteer to host a pregnant girl in their homes while she awaits the birth of her baby.

Idea 12   Surrogate Parents for a Day

It's no secret that many of our kids are growing up in single-family homes, and that even where both parents are present, responsibilities often keep them from giving kids the time and attention they crave. Your church or group can provide a day of fun and meaningful adult time for those kids, as well as give parents a chance to re-energize so they can enjoy their kids upon their return home.

Identify those kids you know who could really use more of an adult presence, for whatever reason. Take a day as a group, and treat those kids to a fun day of activities. Take them to a ball game, an amusement park, or the mall—whatever is most appropriate and enjoyable for your particular group of kids. As much as possible, let the kids themselves choose what activities they'll do. Exercise adult discretion as needed.

Be sure to get parents' permission first. As much as they want to give time to their kids, they'll probably also welcome the idea of several hours of downtime. Be very specific in letting parents know where you'll be and what times you expect to be there—and make a point of keeping to your schedule as much as possible.

Your own church's or group's children can help here as well by being friends and/or accompanying younger kids to activities. But don't let your kids do all the work if you bring them along. *You* make a point of being a friend to these children. And that will probably mean exerting yourself a little more than normal. But it will pay off. Most children don't want to just sit around and talk, but you should have plenty of time to talk "on the fly."

On that note, be sure to bring along plenty of healthy snacks for you and the kids. You're going to need some extra energy today!

Who knows? In some cases, this one-time activity could lead to long-term mentoring relationships by your group members, where they'll commit to pouring their lives into these kids' lives.

After you've returned the kids home (and maybe after giving yourself a little time to recuperate), discuss the following questions:

- What was the most fun part of today for you personally? What was the biggest challenge?

- What insights did you gain into these kids' lives? into how kids think in general?

- Would you be interested in doing something like this again or making a longer-term commitment to one or more of these kids? How?

Idea 13   Life With Hot Flashes

Women have a multitude of questions about "that time of life" but may not have a mother or older friend to ask. Your group can offer help through a day dedicated to informing, encouraging, and supporting.

Schedule a doctor or nurse who specializes in women's health to speak. This medical professional could be from your church or the community. Ask him or her to be prepared to take questions at the end of his or her talk. The suggested time frame for this event should be two to three hours, so be sure to provide refreshments.

Advertise this event in your community newspaper, and highlight the speaker. Emphasize that this is not only a fact-gathering event but also one that will encourage women during this passage of life.

In addition to the main speaker, schedule a woman from your church to speak who is on the other side of menopause. She can give her story of ups and downs but end with encouragement of how the Lord helped her through. Let her take questions, too, if she's willing.

After the speakers finish, your facilitator could ask the women to get into groups of three or four and share for 15 minutes. Then each group could enter a prayer time to pray for specific requests regarding this issue.

In addition to this event, your ministry can set up a support group that would welcome church members and non-members alike for this trying season of life. Prepare a flier about the support group to distribute to the ladies. This gives them an opportunity to talk about the support group before they leave. Announce the support group's first meeting time and place before you dismiss the crowd.

It's important for women to know they're not alone in this time of life and that symptoms eventually will end. Your event will meet the need for information, and your support group will encourage relationships.

Idea 14   Takin' It to the Homeless

If you live in or near even a moderately sized city, you know (or can discover, with a minimum of inquiry) the hangouts where the homeless go during the day when it's still seasonable outside. Instead of having them come to a shelter to meet some of their basic needs, consider stepping out of your comfort zone and going to *their* places to provide help and friendship.

Have your church or group shop for and assemble bags of nonperishable foods. Include juices and water bottles, energy bars, or vacuum-sealed cans of meat or fish, along with napkins and utensils (and can openers, if they'll need them). Make sure foods can be easily chewed, as many homeless people have dental issues that prevent them from eating tougher foods.

You may also want to include personal hygiene items such as soap, shampoo, toothpaste, and toothbrushes. Also, have some New Testaments to give out, so as you share your food, you're also able to share God's Word with them, both verbally and physically.

Idea 15   City Lights

Your church can become known as a helping church in your city, and your men's ministry can take up the charge. Some residents simply cannot do the upkeep on their homes and could use your assistance.

Decide in advance what kinds of jobs your group can and can't do. A men's ministry representative can then call the city and offer to help elderly or disabled residents with house/yard code violations, such as cleaning up after an ice storm or clearing out brush. Stipulate that someone from the ministry would evaluate the job first to see if it is doable. One of your volunteers could meet with the homeowner if possible and talk about how the group could help. If you are unable to make contact with the homeowner, notify the city of the date you'll go look at the job. Decide what it would take to complete the job, and let the city know if and when you plan to take care of the problem.

There are some questions to answer before agreeing to work on a project. What will you do with trash? Will you leave it at the curb or haul it to the dump? Will curbside pickup (or delivering trash to a dumpsite) require a fee? Who will pay it? Is there poison ivy on the property? What is your policy on removing heavy items? Will you do only yard work, or will you consider outside home repairs?

After the job is finished, the ministry should follow up with the city about the job's completion and whether anything was left for the homeowner to take care of, such as trash at the curb. Clarify what you and the homeowner agreed to about the project.

Idea 16   Join a Service Group

Programs for families at risk are found in metropolitan cities around the country. Many denominations and social-service agencies—such as The Salvation Army, Boys & Girls Clubs of America, and both national denominations and local governments—have such programs. These centers provide assistance to families in need, particularly high-risk families. They often provide meals for needy families, and they often have clothing stores where people may purchase items at a low cost.

Consider offering your services to help as needed. Professional skills are always needed—is there a retired lawyer, physician, dentist, or accountant who would be willing to serve? Tutoring children after school, helping prepare a hot meal, or assisting in playground supervision are also tremendous ways to help. Most neighborhood action programs have special events where volunteers are needed. At Christmas they may put on a special Christmas party for children. At Thanksgiving they may offer a Thanksgiving dinner. At Easter they may have a special Easter breakfast.

All of these are wonderful opportunities for servants of Christ to move out of the walls of the church and get involved in the local community.

Idea 17   Christmas Around the World

Spreading the love of Jesus is what we should be all about. There's seldom a better time to do that than the day we celebrate his birth.

Partner with one of the many international organizations out there who are committed to spreading Christmas joy around the world. Samaritan's Purse (www.samaritan.org) and Action International Ministries (www.actionintl.org) are just a couple of such organizations that sponsor projects your group could get involved with.

Spreading Jesus' love by packing shoe boxes for Christmastime is one kind of outreach. Children around the world learn about God's love as they receive shoe boxes filled with basic necessities of life like soap, a comb, a hairbrush, and so on, along with literature that tells kids and adults about the love of Jesus.

Whomever you partner with, make it more than collecting goods for a package. As organizational guidelines allow, pick out items that are extra-special, and write letters to make your love more personal, to both yourself and the receivers of your gifts.

Idea 18 Encouragement Cards

Encouragement cards are another way of helping seniors minister to people both inside and outside the walls of their church. Many seniors are not able to do physical activity, but jotting a few lines of encouragement may be just the thing for someone unable to get involved in projects away from home.

Your church can provide the cards. Have the name and address of the church on the top left-hand corner on the front, and put a Scripture passage on the reverse side, such as Hebrews 10:24-25. Design these cards as simply or elaborately as you like.

Whom the encouragement cards are sent to is up to you, but a good start would be to send cards to those who have little contact with others—such as those in care centers, people under hospice care, or elderly people in skilled nursing-care centers. Encouragement cards could also be sent to neighbors around the church, new people moving into the community, people who have recently been involved in some accident or who have experienced illness, or people in the church who are in need of prayer and encouragement.

Encouragement cards could also be sent to church leadership, ministry servant leaders, church staff, children's workers, youth workers, and even to local government officials. Imagine how the mayor of your city would feel if he or she received an encouragement card from your church. You could send a card to your representatives, to the principal of your high school, or to police officers or firefighters in your area.

Be as creative, and cast as wide a net, as you and your seniors are willing and able to do!

Idea 19 Senior Volunteers

Seniors love to help others, and they have the time, energy, resources, and wisdom to do it well. Actually, many seniors think of volunteering as "payback time"—they've been blessed over the years, and now it's time to give something back.

Nearly every successful organization involves seniors volunteering in some way. Hospitals, care centers, hospice centers, libraries, food banks, and schools all love senior volunteers. There is something about giving and helping that makes people feel good about themselves and takes their minds off of their interests. But there is another benefit to seniors volunteering in local nonchurch efforts: Often they are able to be a witness for Christ and for the church.

A senior volunteering at a hospital may find many opportunities to encourage others. As a patient is being wheeled down a hallway to a waiting room, it is a wonderful opportunity to comfort and encourage. Of course we cannot be preaching or tossing out Bible verses at will, but we can share God's love by our attitude, action, and loving spirit. That could plant a spiritual seed that God may use in the future. It could instill a question, and in answering that question, the volunteer may be able to share God's love in response.

Greeting people at a desk, answering a telephone, guiding others to the chaplain's office or admitting area, serving on a playground at a school, or packing food boxes at a food bank are all opportunities to give words of encouragement.

Also, often when visiting someone in the hospital, care center, or hospice care, the person you're visiting will introduce you to his or her roommate. What a wonderful opportunity to share God's love with a word of encouragement!

Idea 20   Service in Reverse

Nearly every day, someone is there to help us in some way—because it's his or her job. Waitresses, salesclerks, cashiers, Wal-Mart® greeters, day-care or nursing home workers, house cleaners…you've probably thought of someone you know personally (or would like to) already. Why not have your group take an evening to serve those who serve you on a daily basis and give them a much-needed break?

Plan a dinner, and invite six to eight service professionals to be your special guests. Set a formal table. Treat your guests as special, and be genuine about it. Try as much as possible to put yourself in their shoes; talk to them about their jobs and how you appreciate the service they've given you. Also ask about the things that really matter in their lives, and listen as they share.

Make a habit of throwing these dinners, if you like. The service professionals *you* serve will not only feel loved and appreciated, but next time you're dealing with a busy salesclerk or get the wrong order delivered for lunch, you'll see the situation with brand-new eyes!

Idea 21   Keeping Your Eyes Open

Service ideas are everywhere, and it becomes progressively easier to spot them as you keep an eye out for opportunities to live out these "one anothers":

- **Grieving families.** Provide dinner, an activity to help take their minds off their grief for a little while, a listening ear, and relief from the pressure of things that need to be done. Realize that they'll be distracted and distressed, so call to remind them to come on over (or ask if you can go there). Don't try to force them to cheer up. Ask about the loved one who died, and allow them to share stories, even if it happens through tears. Don't worry about offering "the right words" of comfort. Instead, simply express your sorrow over their loss, and offer your love.

- **Families with infants.** Offer to provide meals, housecleaning, lawn mowing, and any other maintenance chores that get pushed aside when a newborn takes precedence. Offer to come and watch the baby at their house for an hour or two so the parents can get some much-needed rest. Find out if the family is lacking in any of the many basic things a baby needs, and provide them.

- **Families who've lost a job.** Straight-out offers of cash are often difficult to accept, so look for other ways of providing for unemployed families' needs. Collect money and buy grocery store gift certificates, gas cards, paper for printing out résumés, and other practical items. Or find some odd jobs they can do to both help them feel more useful and to earn some badly needed cash on their own.

As you prayerfully look for opportunities, be sure that God will bring those opportunities your way and give you the resources and ideas you need to help meet those needs.

Caring for the Long Haul: Ideas for Long-Term Service

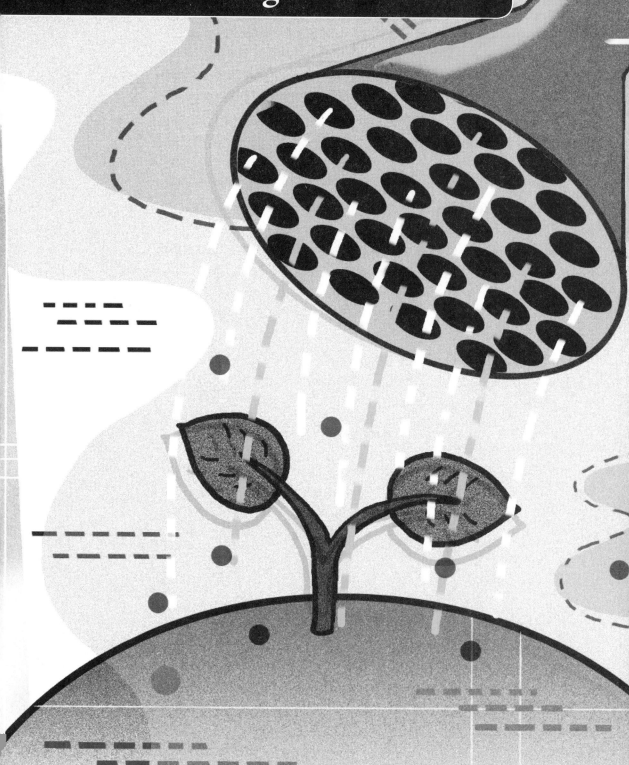

OK—so your church has started getting comfortable with the whole idea of outreach, not to mention the whole idea of finally *doing* some outreach. You've been putting a human face on Jesus' love, in a number of simple, practical ways, and even people who don't know Jesus are beginning to recognize that.

So now it's time to wade out a little farther into the deep end. You're ready to consider making some long-term commitments to those in your community (or even farther out) who really need longer-term help. The ideas in this section are here to help you take those next steps.

Children, teenagers, adults, seniors—there are people in all of these age groups who are just waiting for someone to be there for them. This section will give you ideas on where to find them and what you can do to help them. And as you begin reaching even further out—and sticking it out even when things get tougher—your church, your group, your *lives* will become even more alive and growing in Jesus.

9 Ways to Serve Your Children and Youth

Idea 1   Kids' Service Program

One of the best ways you can serve kids is not by doing something for them but by helping them do something for others. We can serve them by helping them experience the joy and meaning that is found in helping others and by giving them the rewarding experience of being producers, not just consumers, of good.

Create a kids' service program. Most churches have numerous community service projects like helping build houses, serving food for the poor, cleaning up yards for the elderly, or visiting troubled youth. Schools are almost always happy to get kids involved in things like this, and experience in service can even help in getting jobs and scholarships later on. Bring the kids along to watch, and find some parts of these projects that younger kids can do. Give them a chance to contribute and feel ownership of your project.

Make it easy and short, and give the kids a picnic or take them out for ice cream afterward. Have a discussion session, and ask them questions like, "What did you like about the project?" "How was it hard?" "What about the people you helped surprised you?" "Why do these people need help?" and "How could you keep helping them?"

Try to do one project a month for a whole school year. You might want to do this with just one class. You'll need to arrange with the school to promote these projects as service learning excursions. If you handle it right, the school should be happy about it, and the kids will get to have fun and feel like they've done something important for the community. Beyond the immediate benefits, these projects will provide a chance for kids to see what the church *really* does. The friendships and goodwill they experience will give them a positive outlook on the body of Christ.

Idea 2   Tutoring At-Risk Kids

Many children grow up with little support or encouragement from adults. Tragic at all ages, the lack of appropriate role models and mentors has many educational, social, and spiritual consequences. Your adult, young adult, or senior high groups can do something to help.

Contact the guidance counselor of a middle school or high school near your church, and offer to provide free tutoring services. Let the counselor guide you on how to make your services available to the students. Recruit volunteers with education in a variety of subjects, and set a time shortly after school to be available at your church facility.

If your building has a family life center, gym, or other less threatening area, use that for the tutoring center. Have light, inexpensive, and healthy snacks available. Don't overwhelm those who venture in with too much attention.

Be sure to check with your church office about background checks for anyone who works with teenagers, and find out if church policy is adequate for the school whose students you're helping as well. If not, a very useful resource is Group's Church Volunteer Central network (churchvolunteercentral.com), a subscriber-based site that not only contains ready-made background checks and parental consent forms but also many other articles and resources to help recruit, equip, retain, and lead church volunteers.

Follow the school's standards without grumbling or exception, making sure there's no opportunity for negative situations to develop.

You'll spend time helping kids with math and history, but you'll also hear heartbreaking stories about family situations and precarious circumstances. Your numbers may fluctuate wildly, as some students you come to care about may simply stop coming. But keep in mind that you are planting seeds of truth and watering lives with love.

Idea 3   Adventure Sports Program

It can be hard to get high school kids interested in spending time at church. A quarterly adventure sports program is one great way to reach out to nonchurched kids and help develop relationships with them.

Plan an adventure sports outing four times a year, one for each season. What sports you choose will largely be determined by where you live and what resources are available. Here are some ideas: river rafting or canoeing in the summer, rock climbing or hiking in the fall, snowshoeing or skiing in the winter, and geocaching or rappelling in the spring. For some sports, you'll need to secure professional assistance or do them at an indoor facility, as with rappelling and rock climbing.

Have your high school kids invite their friends to these events. They'll want to come—kids love challenges! Promote and advertise these events well before they occur to get kids excited and to keep them coming back. Events could even be weekend trips, which would be a great opportunity to develop even deeper friendships.

Activities like this are a good way to get new kids involved with your church youth group. Aside from big events like these, try to support the long-term effort by doing fun small things as a youth group frequently, like trips to water parks, games of capture-the-flag, and holiday parties. It may also provide opportunities for both on-the-spot or long-term mentoring—keep your eyes and hearts open for such opportunities.

Bear in mind that these adventure experiences can cost a bit. Try to get group rates from outfitters. And make this an opportunity for church members to provide scholarships for kids who wouldn't be able to otherwise come. By investing time and resources in kids this way, you'll not only be providing them with incredible memories and experiences, you'll be connecting them to the church in a way that will make them thirsty to find out more.

Idea 4　**Men to Boys**

Boys need Christian male role models in their lives. Your small group—especially a men's group—can make a difference in boys' lives whose time with Christian men, or men of any kind, may be limited.

Open this ministry to those whose sons or grandsons would benefit from a relationship with a Christian mentor. Meet with your pastor to explain the vision and to ask for his or her input and support. Your ministry can design a flier to explain the mentoring opportunities available and distribute it at church on the Sundays of the announcements. Give a contact name and number to call for more information for parents who want to include their sons in this program.

Volunteers from your group will each set up specific times with the parents to meet with the boys. This is most effective if it is on a regular basis, whether it's once a week or once a month. This is a time for the volunteers and boys to just hang out together. It could be as big as going to a professional baseball game or as small as going to get ice cream. The idea is to spend time together and talk. Over time the relationship can develop into one in which the boy is comfortable in sharing his good times, his problems, or his fears.

Hold a meeting of volunteers to discuss the ministry. You could give them a book on Christian mentoring if you find one that you feel fits your ministry. A great one on this subject is Sam Mehaffie's *Every Man's a Mentor* (Xulon Press). Set a limit to the time commitment—six months to a year is good—so they won't think they must continue volunteering until the boy is grown. (However, relationships *can* develop that will last a lifetime.)

Remind them that this ministry should be based in prayer for the boys and for themselves. They will need God's guidance as they relate to impressionable young boys. Pair volunteers with boys as requests come in.

At the end of your season of mentoring, celebrate with a barbeque or another type of "guy event," and give your boys opportunity to help plan and contribute to your closing event.

Idea 5   Partnering With Special-Needs Parents

Special-needs children are often very loving, welcoming, and caring. However, they struggle in traditional Sunday school programs, where the ratio of adults to children is not in their favor. They sometimes need one-on-one attention, which is not always possible in that environment. Therefore, they end up missing out on Sunday school and child-care programs at the church.

For parents, this is tough. They may struggle taking their special-needs children into the church, and when they do, they probably spend more time focusing on their child than worshipping and growing closer to Jesus.

Agree to regularly take a special-needs child to Sunday school (so parents can go to church without interruption!) or youth group. If your church only has one morning service, find three others to do this with you and take turns missing the service once a month for a year.

It might seem like something that requires official training or education. However, most children who would fall into this category only need a friend for an hour or two who is willing to be right at their side and help guide them. The parents could probably meet with the volunteers to share helpful tips to work with their particular child.

Idea 6   Scholarships

We routinely send money when our youth go off on short-term missions or service trips, don't we? How about making the same commitment to our young adults as they head off for a much longer-term commitment, and into an environment that's often more hostile toward the gospel—*college*?

The years away at college can be hard on a young adult's faith and pocketbook. Your group or church can help on both counts. And although you can go as far as raising cash for courses and books, you can begin helping in much more basic ways as well.

Get a list of college students from your church, and send them care packages at least twice a semester. Include fun things as well as practical items. Homemade snacks and toiletries will be appreciated. Other ideas include rolls of quarters for laundry, fast-food coupons, coffeehouse gift certificates, encouraging cards and letters, church newsletters or bulletins, copies of the local paper with interesting stories about people they know, packets of hot chocolate and a fun mug, and a devotional book or Bible.

Keep a list of all the college kids' e-mail addresses, and send frequent, encouraging e-mails to them. Or send an "e-postcard." Include questions that allow the student to check the right answer or give brief answers. Make it informative as well as humorous. One brief example:

"School is going:

__ Great!

__ OK.

__ What school?

My number-one prayer request is _____."

Don't feel restricted to supporting just your church's kids—by including other area college kids who don't know Jesus, you'll be sending them a powerful message about your love—and Jesus' love—for them.

As you support and stay connected with your college students, you'll be letting them know that someone cares for them and giving them the opportunity to be open about the struggles they're having in these first big steps toward becoming independent adults.

Idea 7   Finals Food…and More!

Studying and snacking seem to go hand in hand. Use exam time as an opportunity to start some longer-term contact time with students.

Start by blessing them with a special treat. Ask for volunteers at your church, who are involved with students or not, to bake as many yummy treats as possible. Package them in small zipper bags, and add a note of encouragement.

The next step is delivery. Gather all your volunteers, and surprise your students with finals food. When you visit, ask them for the name and address of one of their friends in the same boat who doesn't go to youth group or church. Right there and then, have your student call the unknown student to give him or her and the parents a heads-up, and then deliver your treats! If you can, take the student you know to the other student's house to make it a more comfortable and relaxed interaction. Use it as a chance to invite the new student to youth group or church.

Don't limit this to finals time. Make it a habit to visit students. Use any school activities or other activities as an excuse. Know of a big game or meet coming up? Stop by with a sports drink and an energy bar. Do you have a student who recently preformed in a school play or concert? If you make it to the event, write a "bravo" note on a blank CD-R to tell the student that one day, he or she might just have a CD of his or her own. For the student who works many hours, pick up a Frisbee or other toy and stop by, reminding him or her to take some time to play, too.

Continue to serve your students all year—not simply during finals time. However, the academic calendar does help in creating entry points, especially if stepping into students' lives like this is a new experience.

Idea 8   Helping Kids Excel

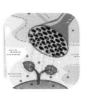

High school, with all of its pressures and the looming possibilities of what comes next, is a hard time. Kids' minds are filled with the prospects of jobs both now and in the future, important tests they'll be taking, and questions about college and what they should study. This is an excellent time to show kids that you care about them and that you want to support and offer them help and guidance through high school and beyond.

A lot of schools have some sort of resource center, with a smattering of helpful information and contacts for students. With a little help from a church group, you can provide much more than that. Make *yourselves* a resource for the kids.

Get as many people as you can in your church to write up a short piece on what kind of work they do or what other kinds of job skills they have, along with contact information, and organize it into a booklet to put in the resource center. Make it informative and practical. That way, kids can find out about things they're interested in and have a contact to find out more or get connected if they need to. If possible, create a Web version, too.

If members have a business with jobs that kids could do and would be interested in, put the members in the booklet. This could also be used as a resource for kids to find cool summer jobs—or more.

Next, create a college resource. As with the job booklet, get people to write informational pieces on the schools they went to and their different majors—what they were like and what was involved—along with contact information so kids can find out more.

With college entrance exams like the SAT and ACT, kids will need help again. You can procure test-preparation books and software from Kaplan or The Princeton Review and provide them to students at a lower cost or for free. You could also see about leading a free weekly seminar for a month on how to do well on these tests by leading kids through one of the prep booklets.

Each of these resources acts as a way of connecting church members to kids; it opens the door for relationships and gives an opportunity for youth to see you as people they can look to for help and guidance whenever they need it. And they'll remember it.

Idea 9   **Liberating Children Around the World**

Your help to children can go beyond those in your neighborhood or even your country, and you can address much more urgent issues while doing so. One especially troubling yet widespread issue finally receiving worldwide attention is that of child sex trafficking, which affects millions of children worldwide—including in the United States. Many children are lured away by false promises; some are sold by relatives; many others are abducted. Your church or youth group can both bring attention to this present-day slavery as well as do something to help.

Consider making a long-term commitment to raising money and awareness for this cause. Among the events or actions you can take are hosting silent auctions, organizing a benefit dinner, or setting up information tables at concerts and summer festivals. Your group could also become a regular sponsor for advocacy, prevention, and aftercare programs, as well as support aftercare workers, safe houses, and socioeconomic development programs in high-risk communities.

A good place to get more information on this subject, as well as information on how you can help, is Justice for Children International (www .jfci.org).

16 Ways to Reach Out to Adults in Need

Idea 1   Life-Skills University

Every community has people who lack basic life skills, and their lives can be significantly improved through classes provided by your church. By offering life-skills classes free at your church, you'll be showing people Jesus' love in equipping them to meet their own needs, and they'll likely be more open to hearing God's message.

Enlist qualified people from your church to teach classes, and advertise widely in your community. If staffing is an issue, consider focusing on the needs of a particular people group in your area, such as non-English-speaking residents or single mothers. You might teach classes on the following: English as a second language, auto maintenance, home maintenance and repair, basic personal or family finances, cooking, conflict management, divorce recovery, or preparing for job interviews.

Avoid using the classes to corner people and pepper them with evangelistic efforts, but be sure to let attendees know what other things your church has to offer. For example, you might give people a printed list of the various services your church offers, including Bible studies, fellowship groups, or compassion ministries. Treat everyone with warmth and kindness, keeping in mind that these classes may be the only connection some people have with a church.

Idea 2   Christ in Culture

Many students from other lands are studying in the United States—and many of them come from countries closed to Christianity. They've come here to get a degree, but while they're here, they also want to experience American culture. Often they're also interested in understanding what Christianity is all about. Unfortunately, most of them will make few friends, and only a tiny percentage will ever see the inside of an American home.

You can minister to international students in a meaningful way by opening your homes and hearts to them, and the holidays are a great time to begin. When college campuses clear out for Christmas break, these young adults who don't have family members nearby often end up spending the winter holiday holed away in an empty dorm room, missing out on the joy and fun of the season. Consider offering to house one or two of them during Christmas break. It's often as simple as contacting a local college's international students office or extracurricular organization.

International students are hungry to learn about American culture—after all, that's why they're here! What better way to learn about a significant part of American culture than by joining a family during their Christmas celebration? In an effort to learn about your culture, most international students—even those from countries that are closed to Christianity—will be very open to participating in and learning about Christian holiday traditions. Sharing openly about holiday customs is a non-threatening way to introduce an international student to your Christian faith.

By opening your home in this way, you'll have a chance not just to offer kindness and friendship to someone who is lonely but also to introduce him or her to the real reason for the Christmas season. Don't be surprised if the winter break with your family is only the beginning of an ongoing cross-cultural friendship!

Take your relationship beyond just the holiday season. Invite your students over during the course of the year, and at the end of the school year, you can celebrate by bringing all of them over for a picnic or cookout!

Idea 3   Pack Up the Van

Especially with rising energy costs, transportation is not just an issue for the elderly anymore. College kids, unemployed adults, or people just struggling to make ends meet are all in need of help. If there's a block of people in your area you know of who need help getting to malls or even to work daily, think about how your church or group could step up to fill that need.

Figure out the logistics of this. Who will be providing transportation? What days and times will you offer these services? Will you need to rotate volunteers? Are safety and liability issues adequately covered?

Once you have a plan, advertise your service(s) in your local paper or on signs around town. Make sure you let people know when you're available. Include a line that says something such as "A free service provided by [group name] at [name of church]" so people will know who you are.

You might have repeat "customers," and they will spread the word to neighbors and friends. As you develop relationships, they may start asking questions about why you're doing this. What a perfect opportunity to invite them to visit your church or group, where they can learn more about a relationship with God!

Idea 4　**Help Wanted**

One group of adults in need who are often overlooked is friends who are struggling with unemployment. Whether they've been fired, laid off, or have decided on their own to quit their job, the often long and lonely process of looking for a new job can be a spiritually exhausting and isolating experience. Not only are unemployed adults facing the immediate stress of paying the bills from a dwindling (or empty) bank account, but they're also dealing with a number of other less obvious issues: feelings of self-doubt and uselessness, confusion about God's leading (or perceived lack of it), injured pride, uncertainty about their vocation, boredom and discouragement, and tension in personal relationships.

People who are struggling with unemployment often need to be ministered to in a unique and sensitive way. Instead of just giving them money (which could worsen their sense of uselessness or cause them to feel that they are accepting "charity"), here's an idea for addressing both their external and internal needs: Invite friends and church members to collaborate by creating a help-wanted list of jobs they'd be willing to pay others to do for them, such as raking leaves, mowing the lawn, babysitting, preparing taxes, grocery shopping, painting a room, tutoring children, cleaning the house, giving children swimming lessons (or helping with another sport), landscaping, house-sitting, pet-sitting, or repairing a roof. Each job listing should include contact info and a specified payment amount.

When friends find themselves unemployed, they can check out the help-wanted list and select jobs they'd like to do. Not only will these jobs provide some extra income, but they will also give those who do the work a sense of usefulness and accomplishment. Providing these types of work opportunities to unemployed adults is often better than simply offering financial assistance, because it helps to combat feelings of boredom, loneliness, injured pride, and despair. And by doing the legwork of coordinating a list of jobs ahead of time, you're helping others avoid the embarrassing experience of calling friends and "begging" for work to do. By compiling help-wanted tasks in a practical list, you can enable those who do the work to maintain a sense of personal dignity while simultaneously addressing at least some of their financial needs.

Idea 5   Money Ministry

We don't need to look at the statistics to realize that a large percentage of people today are in financial trouble—all we have to do is look at people in our churches and neighborhoods. These problems often come because no one ever helped these folks learn how to gauge their income and expenses by creating a budget. Your church can help meet these adults' needs by setting up a money management ministry.

Let your community know about this service by advertising it through both free and paid avenues. Also contact organizations who help families in crisis, or other potential participants, and let them know this service is available.

Through this ministry, you can set up financial mentors—for instance, enlist one couple or individual to mentor each couple or individual who signs up to receive help. This ministry can especially be valuable to folks who are in deep debt or to those who simply don't know the first thing about money management.

Your ministry can have several levels. On the first level, mentors can make sure that "mentorees" understand bills and checkbooks. Participants should bring their financial information with them, so mentors can help them set up budgets.

For some participants who really need help, such as those in debt, mentors can act as financial advisors, helping those they mentor make financial and purchase decisions. If a person is in debt, the mentors can help set up a payment plan to reduce and eliminate the debt.

Some churches even take this kind of financial advising to another level for those who are truly in financial trouble and desperate for help. In those circumstances, the mentor can keep the checkbook and credit cards for the couple, setting up regular times to help them pay bills. The mentor can even shop with the couple to encourage them and teach them how to spend wisely.

Your financial ministry could also expand in another direction—helping seniors and low-income families or individuals, as well as those who participate in your money management program, to do their taxes. Especially if their tax information is pretty straightforward, TurboTax and other programs make taxes simple enough for non-accountants to do!

Idea 6 Businessmen's Roundtable

Not only the poor need our help. The old adage, "It's lonely at the top," applies to Christian entrepreneurs or CEOs who daily are faced with the realities of trying to reconcile their Christian values to the realities of the business world. Your church can set up a businessmen's roundtable to offer these men fellowship with peers as well as help for solving problems in their businesses. You can also provide a safe, noncompetitive environment with other Christian men—as well as to those businessmen who don't know Jesus and couldn't even conceive of an idea like this, but who sorely need it. (You could easily do this for business*women* as well—but as the challenges differ, it's best to hold it as a separate meeting.)

Get started by talking with entrepreneurs and CEOs in your church family about this idea. A business could host a breakfast or lunch once a month, and food and drink do not have to be elaborate (although it should be done well). Set up a schedule for the meetings, publicize them in your church and at businesses and corporations in your town, and encourage members to invite business leaders from outside your church. Plan a short devotional for the beginning of the meetings. Another responsibility your church can take is to send out e-mail reminders one week before each meeting.

Meetings should be about an hour long. A volunteer from your church can facilitate the meeting, or the host can assume that role. After a short devotional and prayer, the men will get their food so they can eat during the remainder of the meeting. Go around the table and give each man an opportunity to discuss a problem he is facing. The other men can counsel him and offer solutions.

The next month the men will report back on the actions they took and the result. This last piece provides accountability for these men who may have no one else to answer to.

Many issues can arise, but here are some sample topics for a meeting: What should you do when a relationship with a customer or supplier sours? How do you handle a faithful employee whose work production changes either in volume or quality? What if the majority of your workers, who are immigrants with legal work permits, cannot get their work papers renewed?

This ministry can be a blessing and a boost to business leaders who often don't have anyone else to talk with who is in their same position.

Idea 7   Minister to the Ministers

Workers at a food closet or homeless shelter give of themselves in service every day. Your church can bless these workers on a regular basis by providing lunch and a needed breather for them.

Consider starting with a monthly commitment. You'll need two teams for the day of the outreach. One team would take the workers' places by serving those coming for food, answering the phone, and performing other regular services. The second team serves lunch to the workers.

The first team will not only serve the people coming in, but they will also talk with them and show interest in them. This team can also do any cleanup needed after serving their guests. The volunteers on this team might need prior training to fill the workers' jobs. Set that up with the shelter before beginning the luncheons.

The second team is there to minister to the workers themselves. Volunteers not only serve food and clean up, but they also offer to pray for the workers' personal needs. They should pray for ministry needs, too.

This outreach will help your church form a relationship with the food closet or homeless shelter, and your willingness to serve those less fortunate will bless both them and you. You can form several teams and take turns going on this outreach, and it would be a good one for your youth ministry to join in the summer.

Idea 8   Church Auto Shop

Do you have some mechanics in your church—or at least guys who feel comfortable around cars? Consider starting a ministry where your professional *and* amateur mechanics can help others in need.

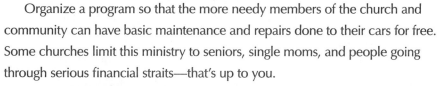

Organize a program so that the more needy members of the church and community can have basic maintenance and repairs done to their cars for free. Some churches limit this ministry to seniors, single moms, and people going through serious financial straits—that's up to you.

You might organize it so that one Saturday a month, those receiving the benefits of this ministry can make appointments to have servicing done at the church or the designated location. Making people set up appointments will help the day stay organized. You might also need to recruit someone to act as organizer and receptionist, because if there's a large demand it will make things go a lot more smoothly. You might also consider limiting clients—for instance, not allowing someone to get servicing done every month, but once a quarter.

Depending on the skills of your church members and the equipment you have available, you can offer various services: oil change, general checkup, tire pressure check, tire rotation, putting more oil or washer fluid in the car, and even putting Freon in air conditioning systems.

You can have training days for guys and gals who may want to serve in this ministry but don't have the mechanical skills—you don't have to teach them the skill-intensive procedures, but you can still teach them the simple maintenance things. This would also be useful training for those you help, so they can become more self-sufficient with their own vehicles.

If you want the ministry to be a long-term service in the community, you might even set up a car barn and equip it with the right kinds of tools. Also talk to those who manage local garages about sending people your way when they can't afford garage services.

Keep people's cars running, and they not only will love you for helping keep them safe and on the road, but they won't have a broken car as an excuse not to come to church!

Idea 9   Community Health

Do you have doctors and nurses in your church? You don't have to wait until disaster-relief situations to give them a ministry—set up something in your church. With health care becoming such an expensive and difficult field, your church can minister to members and those in the community by offering some limited health services.

What you can do is dictated by the kinds of health professionals you have in your church. But consider these areas of service:

- **Healthy heart services.** Offer periodic blood pressure screenings for your church and community members. You can help people understand what their blood pressure is all about—what are safe areas, and when they should see their doctors about controlling their blood pressure. You can give them information on preventive diets and actions. You might consider offering blood pressure screenings as a regular service for seniors and others.

- **Ask a nurse.** You might offer a "clinic day," in which you gather your doctors and nurses to be available to answer any medical questions people might have during individual appointments. Of course, this would not cover in-depth problems, nor would it take the place of a doctor's visit. However, it can still be a valuable service to your members. One main complaint is that doctors don't have enough time to truly listen to the concerns people have. This can give them a chance to voice their concerns with someone who will take the time to listen. And the medical team can also help people prepare the right questions to ask their doctors.

- **Clinic services.** Perhaps your church can host a flu-shot day or a clinic day to help kids get their immunizations before going back to school. Or you might want to contact the community blood bank and plan regular blood donor drives.

- **Provide health-education classes.** Offer an evening seminar on how to have a healthy heart or to explain what diabetes is all about. These can be led by your medical team, or offer your church as a location for hospitals to hold community lectures.

Any and all of these services can be done as a partnership with your local health services clinic, doctors' offices, or hospitals. If anyone in your church works or volunteers at these places, ask that person whom to contact. Otherwise, if the hospital or organization has a volunteer director, talk to that person. In a private office, talk with an office administrator. Tell the person your church is interested in serving the community, and ask him or her how your church can serve with his or her organization.

As you partner with health services already established in your community, you'll not only be helping church members and community members, you'll also be building good relationships with services already in the community.

Idea 10   Women Encouragement Partners

As women go through various seasons of life, they meet many challenges. They need women who have passed through each season to encourage and sometimes advise them. An encouragement partner can relate her experiences—successes *and* failures—at different stages and in different circumstances of life. She can testify to God's presence and help through it all and can describe lessons she learned from the tough times. An encouragement partner could listen to the woman in need, pray with her, and discuss options.

Four groups to consider targeting are newlyweds, new moms, moms of teens, and women approaching menopause.

Announce the ministry in your church. Explain the purpose of the ministry, and plan a group kick-off meeting. Mention that the women in need of encouragement should invite other friends in the community who show interest in such a ministry. Also, inform ladies that this ministry is limited in time—for example, that it will meet twice a month for six months or a year.

Kick off your ministry with a continental breakfast and a devotional for your encouragers. Showcase biblical examples of encouragement and advice, such as Ruth and Naomi, or contemporary examples from someone's personal experience. Explain the ground rules. Include things like confidentiality, keeping it prayer-based, and faithfulness in meeting. Next, take the women who have expressed interest in meeting with a mentor, and with a great deal of prayer, match up each participating woman with a mentor.

The mentors will be able to help women to work through whatever stage of life they're in, and more importantly, as they share, to show them how to become grounded in their relationship with God.

Idea 11   Child-Care Co-Op

Moms of young children need a break. And they need a safe place for their children so they can take a break with confidence that they will be well cared for. Here's your chance to serve these moms!

Set up a co-op for child care. Recruit caretakers who will offer reliable, loving, and safe care. Establish parameters for using the co-op and expectations of both caregivers and moms using the service. Include a reward program for the child-care volunteers to add to the fun and to offer incentives to them.

Once your program is in place, make arrangements for volunteers to touch base regularly with moms outside your co-op program. Young moms don't only need a break—they need advice and often reassurance that they're doing better than they think they are. And sometimes they just need to hear another adult voice. You can be there for them as well as direct them to the God who is always ready to listen and answer their prayers.

Idea 12   Post-Abortive Counseling

Many women who have had abortions feel shame and hide this burdensome, dark secret—even, or perhaps especially, in the church. This is a quiet, rather hidden ministry, but it is a necessary one. You can help break the bondage these women experience through the grace and love of Jesus.

A ministry to these women is probably best headed by another woman (or women) who has experienced deliverance from the shame of abortion. She's been where they are and knows freedom from grief, guilt, and despair. She can assure other women that God loves them and walk them through the necessary steps to receive his forgiveness and to forgive themselves. Counseling and Bible study can be done in a group or on an individual basis. You must assure women that they may remain anonymous, and whatever they discuss will be kept in confidence.

This outreach can be to hurting women throughout your community as well as to your local church body. Ask to talk with the pastor or head of women's ministry in other churches as well, so you can describe your purpose and vision. Notify local pro-life organizations of your ministry, too, in order to reach outside the church.

Your local pregnancy resource center will have useful information on counseling post-abortive women. It can also refer you to national ministries and other resources.

Base your ministry in prayer, and expect the women to become whole. This ministry should be limited in time rather than going on forever. Design a several-week program that has an end. The women should go from taking responsibility through the steps of grief to forgiveness and wholeness. However, if this limited program is not enough, direct the group or individuals to long-term counseling as needed.

Idea 13   Caring for Widows, of Any Age

Recently widowed women are often overwhelmed by the responsibilities that have now fallen to them alone. Many issues face a woman after the death of her spouse. Your church can come alongside her and help ease the burden.

Form a ministry of men and women who will commit to widows for as long as they are needed—maybe even for life, if your group agrees to such a commitment. If a widow is unsure of how to get insurance money or settle the estate, a knowledgeable volunteer can guide her in steps to take and whom to contact. Some women never handled finances in a marriage and are overwhelmed with the checkbook, charge accounts, and taxes. If the woman is uncomfortable with anyone seeing her finances, recommend trusted professionals.

Yardwork and home repair are two more areas that can seem almost impossible to deal with for a woman who was never been primarily responsible for either. Ask your youth ministry to help in these areas.

A volunteer should contact the widow a few weeks after her husband's death and gently offer help. Tell her about services you can perform, and ask her what she needs immediately. She may express gratitude and relief to get help. Yet you may come across a woman who refuses your help because of independence, fear of imposing on others, or fear of being taken advantage of. Give her a name and number to call if she changes her mind, and check back with her in a month or so. Don't be a nuisance; just remain willing to serve. After several weeks of carrying this load alone, she may decide to accept help after all.

Ask one of the women volunteers to call this widow to pray with her. Tell her to feel free to call for prayer or just to talk. If she doesn't, call her back in a few weeks, and pray with her again.

Other women can meet the new widow for coffee or lunch when she is ready to get out. Two or three ladies can take turns meeting with her every few weeks. However, one of them may form a strong relationship with her and will continue the ministry alone.

A widow can feel paralyzed after her husband's death, so volunteers who take the initiative and call about possible services are a blessing. Don't be pesky, but let her know you care and that she is not alone.

Idea 14   "Remember My Chains…"

In closing his letter to the church in Colosse, the imprisoned Apostle Paul tells the church, "Remember my chains" (Colossians 4:18). Paul faced loneliness, despair, physical confinement, and worse as a prisoner for the gospel. He found great comfort in the love, support, and prayers of his Christian brothers and sisters.

Prisoners today—especially those without the vibrant relationship with Jesus that Paul had—are similarly lonely, hurting, and stigmatized by society. They've been branded as criminals, are paying a painful price for the guilt of their wrong actions, and have been cast away by society. Is redemption even *possible* for someone in that situation?

Yes!

Jesus began his earthly ministry in Nazareth by declaring, "He has sent me to proclaim that captives will be released" (Luke 4:18). Even those who are incarcerated can experience the inner freedom and forgiveness Jesus provides through a relationship with him. Christians can live counterculturally by *caring* about those in prison—by seeing them as real people and reaching out to offer them real hope.

Prison ministry groups offer plenty of volunteer opportunities for Christians to minister to those who are in prison, such as by regularly visiting and building relationships with prisoners (under the guidance of a ministry group or a chaplain), by providing practical help to children of incarcerated parents, through written correspondence, and through regular prayer.

A few organizations where you can find more information about this critical ministry are Prison Fellowship (www.prisonfellowship.org), International Network of Prison Ministries (www.prisonministry.net), and Bible Believers Fellowship, Inc. (www.prisonministry.org).

Idea 15   Weekly Trade Sheet

Instead of selling things you no longer want, use them to help the haves and have-nots connect, in your church and beyond.

Print a "purple sheet" each week, where those in your church can see what others may be looking for or trying to sell or give away. You could also charge your church users a small amount for advertising—with the money going toward missions.

To enhance outreach in the community, distribute these sheets at "freebie racks" and bulletin boards in grocery stores, libraries, and other public places. Or talk to the city council about your church putting your information on a Web page that helps community members connect.

Another way to help people connect is to have a bulletin board on which members can list items for sale or items needed. If you choose this option, you might ask someone to be responsible for cleaning the bulletin board periodically—checking to see if needs are met after a couple of weeks. Put it in an easy-to-access area of your church, and let others in your community know they're free to stop by and check this church bulletin board—and even to post their needs on it.

Of course, you can also have an electronic bulletin board on your church Web site—preferably in a members-only area to protect members' privacy. Or have a church trade day, when people set up booths or tables with items to sell or give away. For visibility, you can even do it as a "swap meet" in the church parking lot. To use these mediums to further help those in the community, partner with shelters and crisis-pregnancy centers to advertise their needs to your members.

Idea 16   Disaster Help

Despite the fact that you'd rather not meet others this way, disasters offer tremendous opportunities to show the love of Jesus to broken, bewildered, and hurting people. Your church can reach out in tangible ways, such as taking in food and water, helping to repair or rebuild damaged homes or churches, or outfitting children for school.

The next time the news reports a disaster locally or nationally, your church leaders should pray about offering help. Determine your focus before going to the disaster area. What kinds of needs will you meet, and do you have the skills and resources available for such a project? It's important to define the scope of your project so that the devastation does not overwhelm volunteers when they go to the targeted area.

First, find a church or ministry to work with in the disaster area. This can be done through people in your church or through other ministries you know. Second, send a small team to the area to meet with those contact people. Find out what's currently being provided and what else needs to be done. You may need to help the ministry with repairs first so that it can operate efficiently and so you can have a base of operations.

The small team will assess the area and decide if any of the needs fit your church's focus. A project must have the senior pastor's approval and enthusiastic support to get manpower and funds for it. In addition, define the parameters of the project and its goal in order to know when it is completed.

Set up a schedule of working trips into the disaster area, and publicize the dates. Your members may find co-workers or students who would like to help you even though they are not Christians—welcome them to work alongside you and to take part in any praise services or prayer times you conduct.

Specify the kind of work volunteers will do, and furnish on-the-job training if necessary. In addition, ask them to pray with people or just listen to them and form relationships as they meet their material needs.

Disaster relief affords your church an occasion to serve suffering people. In addition, a great side benefit is the bonding that happens among your people—Christian and non-Christian alike—as they work together for an extended time toward a common goal.

5 Ideas for Caring for Seniors

Idea 1   Adopt a Grandparent

Elderly people go through a range of different experiences and emotions when they reach a point in their lives where they need ongoing medical and life care. Sometimes they feel as if their independence has been taken away— a challenge to anyone's self-esteem. Sometimes they feel abandoned or alone, particularly if their families live elsewhere. Yet volunteers at such care facilities will usually find very receptive guests.

As a group, adopt an elderly individual or couple—or more, depending on the size of your group. Find someone who is unable to get around very well and who needs some help and companionship. Look for someone who doesn't have a lot of family in the area.

Organize a group to regularly visit a retirement home in your community. Often such facilities already have a system for using volunteer help. Gather your group beforehand to encourage them to think about what people experience when they move into an assisted living facility. Discuss God's concern with those who are in need or ignored. Discuss why we are called to take care of those who have nothing material to offer us in return. Throughout the Old Testament, God held the Israelites accountable for the way they treated widows, orphans, and foreigners living within their territory. Prophets such as Amos chastised the Jewish people whenever they neglected those among them who couldn't defend themselves. God wants us to pay attention to those who are ignored by a society of wealth and advancement.

When you begin your visits, ask the facility how you can be of most use; chances are, they'll be ready with an answer. You might be asked to lead a bingo game, visit people who cannot leave their beds, or play music.

Throughout the year, provide services for your adopted senior. There may be other services you can provide inside the house, such as moving furniture or doing any cleaning the senior is unable to do alone. You can also plant flowers, bake cookies, or prepare a meal. Some members of your group could volunteer to be on call either to take your adopted senior to the store, doctor, or church, or to run errands.

Don't get so wrapped up in chores, however, that you forget the aspect of companionship. Encourage your volunteers to take time out from their tasks to engage in conversations with your adopted senior(s). Also be sure to send birthday and holiday cards. Show them you're thinking of them, even when you're not there.

Idea 2   Shepherding Groups

Most churches have a small-group ministry of some sort. Expand the scope of that ministry by holding a specialized small group (or groups) designed specifically for senior adults.

Find a volunteer who would be willing to receive training in how to be a shepherd group coordinator, and sit down with him or her beforehand to discuss the possibilities for this ministry.

Most senior groups would need to meet during the day, and you would need to consider geographical location and transportation. You might have some groups for your seniors who would like serious Bible study; other groups for seniors who are looking for more fellowship; and other groups for trips, excursions, eating out, or whatever creative ideas come to mind. Give your group a name—it helps give personality to the group.

Providing helpful resources is another must. Whatever you decide, have a simple, clear purpose for your shepherd group (or groups) and communicate exactly what you are offering. More ideas for senior groups can be found in *Senior Adult Ministry in the 21st Century: Step-By-Step Strategies for Reaching People Over 50* by David P. Gallagher (Wipf and Stock).

Idea 3   Senior Spa Day

If you live in a metropolitan area, chances are you have a nursing home within a stone's throw of your church. And while churches often minister in nursing homes during the Christmas season, how about the other 11 months of the year? Especially with the mobility of society today, people in nursing homes tend to be lonely. Often they have no family nearby. And as their hands become less limber, sometimes they are not able to take care of grooming as they'd like—and that can be discouraging.

Your church can minister in nursing homes by having a Senior Spa Day once or twice a month—do it with whatever regularity you'd like, but set it up as a regular offering so seniors can count on it happening on certain days. Arrange with the nursing home staff to set up days when seniors can make appointments for free facials, manicures, pedicures, and even haircuts or perms.

What an opportunity for those with cosmetology talents to have a ministry outlet! And those who may not be so gifted can still give manicures and paint fingernails and toenails!

Set up a sign-up sheet in the nursing home, making times available for whatever services you can provide. Before giving services, you might have the nursing home administrator check the names and OK the services. Some clients may have medical conditions that would prohibit their enjoyment of some of the services. For instance, a nonmedical person generally cannot give a pedicure to a person with diabetes.

Put out a call in the church for members to provide perm or hair color kits or fingernail polishes. You might even be able to get donations of some of these items—and equipment like emery boards and nail clippers.

Create a warm, fun atmosphere—perhaps bring along a stereo with CDs of hymns and fun Christian music as a background witness. Let nursing home clients know your church is doing this service out of love. At some point, you may even want to provide transportation for some of them to come to your church. But even if they don't, know that with your attention and physical touch, you're loving people like Jesus would and giving them something to anticipate for days!

If you do this service multiple times a month, you could break it up to have a separate manicure day or pedicure day. You could even host classes showing the seniors the latest new fashions in fingernail polish, or you could encourage them to invite their granddaughters to come learn how to do French manicures. Since seniors love mail and don't get enough of it, set up a system to send your regular "clients" a reminder of the day when you'll be there. Then, look for other ways your church can be part of these seniors' lives on a regular basis.

 ## Idea 4   Hospital Sitters

A powerful way to care for seniors is to train and equip a team of servant leaders who are ready at a moment's notice to go to the hospital to sit with family members when someone is having surgery.

Most hospitals would welcome this support. The hospital chaplain is a good person to see to share your idea. He or she can guide you in how to get this sort of program going. Be sure your goal is not to preach to people, but rather to be an encouragement during their time of need. This also relieves the pastor or staff members from sitting through the entire surgery. The pastor or staff person might suggest that a family member or hospital sitter contact him or her as soon as the doctor gives any update.

It is amazing to see the impact made upon the person in surgery knowing that such caring is being offered—as well as upon family members who see this care being given.

Idea 5   Telecare Ministry

Telecare ministry is a practical way to care for seniors. Active and inactive seniors alike may participate in this ministry, and it may be used to reach people both within and outside of the church.

Names and addresses of first-time church guests or people who have recently moved into the community may be used. The chaplain at a local hospital may provide names of people admitted who have no family or church home. The local mortuary may provide the names of people who have recently lost a loved one and who have no church connection; often the local newspapers are helpful sources of information as well.

A telecare ministry calling report form should include the name of the person to be contacted along with his or her telephone number. There also could be a note of how often the call should be made—weekly, bimonthly, or monthly. A bit of background about the reason or need for the call should also be given, and space should be provided for the date the call was made, the caller's name and comments, and prayer requests or praises. Telecare ministry calling reports should be turned in to either the pastor, associate pastor, or whoever is coordinating the ministry.

Telecare ministry is an amazingly effective way for caring for seniors—or for that matter, anyone in the church. There could even be a ministry established where all seniors in need are telephoned daily just to be sure they are safe.

AT the end of the gospel of Matthew, Jesus tells his disciples—and by extension, all Christians—"[G]o and make disciples of all the nations…Teach these new disciples to obey all the commands I have given you" (Matthew 28:19-20). Most of us know the command. What we *don't* always know is how to make the importance of reaching those we've never seen real enough that it becomes the passion it really ought to be. So what are some steps you can take to develop that passion?

The ideas here will help you understand the significance of missions—and more importantly, give you ways to become more connected with those who *have* gone out into the world. And there are even some ideas on how you can develop your *own* missions trips.

So go ahead—expand your horizons to the ends of the earth—it's what Jesus tells us to do! The ideas here will help you make it a reality.

7 Ideas for Mission Trips

Idea 1   Mission Trip to the Missionaries

If your church supports missionaries abroad, send a small team to each missionary to be their servants for a week. The hard work of a few people can be a huge encouragement to a fellow worker and really ease their burdens.

Servant duties can include:

- **Spring cleaning:** Scrub the toilets; scrub the bathtub; clean out the fridge. You get the idea.

- **Shopping:** Take over market duty for the week.

- **Cooking:** Who wouldn't want their own personal chef for a week? Pack lunches and make their favorite dishes for dinner. And don't forget to do the dishes.

- **Any other chores that need to be done:** This is a great opportunity to tackle the big jobs that might be neglected otherwise, like repairing fences or cleaning out gutters—ask them what they need.

Before beginning to plan, make sure this trip is something the missionary would be interested in. Once there, respect the time and privacy needs of the missionaries. They may already be taxed to the max, and gabfests until midnight might not be their idea of refreshment. Be perceptive to how much social interaction they would like, and establish a schedule before the trip.

Also, don't be thinking "Woo-hoo—free lodging for my adventure trip!" This isn't a chance to make those travel dreams come true. Provide for your own housing. The idea is to be a help, not a houseguest.

After the trip, your servants can be ambassadors to the church back home. While on the trip, have them take pictures, listen to stories, and find out how things are going. Upon returning home, they can share what they saw and rally the church to continued prayer and support for the missionaries. You may want to have them share at church, in a small group, or at a special event. After they've told their stories, break your congregation or group into subgroups of four and discuss these questions:

- Which story told tonight is the most encouraging to you? Why?

- Why is serving others such a blessing to ourselves, ultimately?

- What's one thing you can do personally to serve others each week?

Idea 2   Form a Bond With a Sister Church

If you want to encourage and be encouraged, form a long-term relationship with a church in another country. Your denomination may be able to help pair you with a suitable church abroad. Here are some ideas you and your sister church could do together:

- Send mission teams to the sister church, if it's financially possible. The mission teams can stage a vacation Bible school, do construction work the church may need, or minister to the sister church's community.

- Commit to pray for one another. Send prayer lists to one another that will be communicated to each congregation. These lists could be sent monthly or biannually, depending on how easy communication is for the sister church.

- Form pen pal friendships between the children of the two congregations. Children will make new friends and learn what Christian life is like in another country. Language may be a barrier, but many international kids do have basic English skills. It might be a good chance for them to improve their English skills and for American kids to start learning a new language.

- Share what God is teaching you. How encouraging would it be to hear what God is doing in the lives of people thousands of miles away? Send tapes or CDs of recent sermons or written notes.

- Send care packages containing regional items and pictures of your congregation, if finances allow. There may be small items that kids from the sister church would just love to get their hands on, and vice versa.

Make sure that the goal of the relationship is *mutual* edification. Your church might be surprised how much it can learn from a tiny church in an obscure village. Approach the relationship with the attitude that you both want to encourage, support, and learn from one another. (It's not a one-way "church reaching out to help a poor church" thing.)

The strong bond that can be formed between churches can be a powerful source of prayer, friendship, and encouragement for years to come!

Idea 3　Across the Age Barrier

Next time you and your students plan a youth missions trip, invite the entire church. Yes—the entire church. Gather your students and suggest that instead of making your service opportunity age specific, it's open to people of all ages. This is a fantastic way to break the age barriers and build multigenerational relationships in your congregation.

Pick a site that can handle everyone from young children to senior citizens. Tasks can be anything from heavy manual labor to helping with cooking duties. Having a variety of people around could open the door to a variety of ways to provide service at your destination. Work with the organization to find housing. Make sure that it would be safe for people of all ages and not so uncomfortable that the elderly would be unable to go.

Build work teams involving people from all stages of life. This will help show the different generations of the church the value of learning from each other. It's OK to have some age-specific activities, such as during free time or small groups, but even mixing up those can be a blessing. Ask families to drive, if possible, to cut down on transportation costs. They might have vans and SUVs that can hold all of them plus a few others. Encourage families to go on this "vacation with a purpose" instead of a traditional getaway.

Promoting this from within the youth ministry will give your students a chance to shine and show the congregation how incredible they are. It will make a significant impact on the community you serve as your people bring an entire church body to share God's love.

Idea 4　How the Other Half Lives

Many of us are sheltered from the harsh realities of life. Arrange for your church or group to go on a short-term trip to one of the poorer neighborhoods in your city or in a nearby city. This experience will give you some experience in the way others live.

A two-week summer trip could be ideal. Plan several months ahead so you'll have the resources you'll need, such as tools, transportation, and money. Have a sign-up sheet at church, and have your pastor champion your upcoming project during worship so that everyone can get involved if they choose to do so. It would also be ideal if participants in this experience can find accommodations somewhere in the immediate vicinity for the duration of this project.

Identify the areas of need you'll be meeting—physical and spiritual—and ways that you'll meet those needs. Groups can get involved in the following:

- **Building or repairing homes.** Most churches have people who are very good at this. Those who do not have these gifts can still provide basic assistance for those who want to be involved here.

- **Leading Bible studies.** There are always some people who are gifted in this area of need. Don't forget to arrange for an interpreter, if you're working in a particular ethnic area. Use more universal symbols or pictures where possible.

- **Organizing games with the kids.** Take a ball and other little things that may help. Church members can be encouraged to help with collecting the materials they may need. These could include crayons, chart paper, flannel graph pictures, craft scissors, and so on.

- **Addressing—and experiencing—hunger.** If you really want to begin to understand what poor people go through regularly, miss a meal or two before you meet with them. Even better, provide them with meals while you give up that meal. The joy of watching others having the basics will help us be grateful to God for the meals we have every day. (Here's something to think about and discuss later: What does the smell of good food do to you when you don't have access to food? Imagine what the poor go through daily with empty stomachs.)

Everybody should be involved in sharing the love of Jesus, with both your actions and your words. Use available forums like evening meetings to share gospel stories and get the community exposed to the good news of Jesus. Share one-on-one where possible. Make friends. These are people just like you!

On your return, arrange for a reflection session at your church. Display the pictures you took on your trip during a Sunday morning or evening service, and discuss the following:

- Tell about an incident that touched your heart. What impressed you the most? What made you sad?

- What was it like to be hungry? What did this teach you about the people you were working with?

- How did you go about sharing the love of Christ in this community?

• How can your church be involved on a long-term basis in helping this community?

Idea 5   Nowhere to Lay Their Heads

A great percentage of the world's poor live on the streets day in and day out. Develop your understanding of this by starting closer to home. Speak with the staff of a local homeless shelter or rescue mission and arrange for your group to spend several days to a week at their shelter. Get involved, and stay there overnight (rather than off-site) if that's possible.

Help in the daily work at the shelter while you are there. Find out from the staff what areas could use your help, then get involved. Offer to help residents with whatever can realistically be done. Get involved in listening to their stories, and share the gospel where possible in individual or group situations.

After your service period, reconvene at your church and discuss and prepare a hierarchy of needs that you saw at the shelter or mission. Put the final version on a whiteboard for all to see. Then discuss the following questions:

• What was the experience of being in the shelter like for you?

• Think of your own basic needs from the bottom to the top. How do your needs differ from those of the people you served?

• How can we continue to share the love of Jesus in ways that are meaningful to them? How does helping them with their basic needs open them up to hear the good news of Jesus?

Idea 6   Crossing the State Line

Get involved in a two- to three-week assignment in a neighboring state where people are living under poor conditions. Set an example while being blessed by the experience yourself.

Work out an arrangement with the local pastor in the community you'll be involved with. He or she will know the community well. This can be done in two stages with a couple of weeks between your exploratory stage and the involvement stage.

First meet with the pastor, and go on visits with him or her throughout the community. Let him or her take the initiative in identifying the specific needs of the children and teens (or even adults or families, if you want to broaden your involvement).

Then, take a week or two in between to prepare and collect food items, tools, and whatever else you'll need to make this trip a success. Arrange for a team of adults, or young people with adult supervision, to go out and live in that community.

Then get involved alongside the local church. Offer to sit with the children and teens of that neighborhood and help them with basic skills such as reading, writing, and arithmetic. The children may also need books to read and toys to play with. Distribute food, powdered milk for the children, or canned goods where needed. Help young mothers with basic information on how to take care of their infants, and provide basic health and hygiene care.

Church volunteers can also take turns helping with other needs that were identified during your exploratory stage, such as repairing homes and ministering to those who are ill. Keep your eyes open for opportunities to present the gospel while meeting basic needs.

After this time of involvement, regroup back at your home church and discuss the following:

- What did you learn about other people in need through this project? How did it change your perceptions about peoples' needs?

- What feelings did you have as you got more involved?

- How did the needs you saw compare with those in your own community?

- What specific steps will you take in the future to help others in need?

Idea 7   Senior Missions Trip

More and more churches are realizing that senior adults have the time, resources, energy, and expertise to handle even the more challenging of missions trips. When seniors go on a short-term mission trip, they join with other Christians and begin to live God's love in a way many never dreamed possible. As teams work together and reach out with compassion, they gain the trust and friendship of those they help, allowing them to share God's love in a natural, effective way.

Seniors involved in short-term mission projects can plan on laughing and learning like never before. It will take them out of their comfort zone, but most active senior adults actually want that. After the novelty of cruises and travel wears off, seniors tire of earthly pleasures and want more meaning in their retirement.

Those able to travel will find the idea of traveling for a worthy project extremely interesting. New friends are made, often with people of a different culture. Most trips involve equal portions of hard work and ministry to children through kids' clubs and other types of outreach ministries.

There is also culture shock. Sometimes there are unrealistic expectations and team conflicts. But the growth that takes place in the life of any senior who participates in a short-term mission trip is staggering. Most denominations can put seniors in touch with short-term mission coordinators.

13 Creative Ways to Support Missions

Idea 1   Special-Ops Team

If you ask people in the missions field, they won't hesitate to tell you some of their biggest needs: money, money, and money. Sometimes simply maintaining the support necessary to keep their heads above water takes all their energy—which leaves them with nothing to provide the little extra touches that refresh them spiritually.

Form a special-ops team that can seek out, target, and alleviate the special needs missionaries may have—whether it's in the field or while they're on furlough. Here are some good special-ops targets:

- Plan a spiritual retreat. This could be a visit to a monastery, a fishing trip, or a few days on a beach.

- Give them a book or scholarship for a financial seminar or class, such as Financial Peace University (www.daveramsey.com/fpu/home). This can be an especially helpful resource for those constantly grappling with a lack of funds.

- Get them a gym membership, if that's usable in their area of the world.

- Sponsor their attendance at a ministry conference—or a marriage conference (if it's a couple).

- Give them a gift certificate or money for a special night out.

What you give will largely depend on their tastes and their current setting (urban or rural), but giving special gifts several times a year will refresh and bless these servants!

Idea 2   Basket Cases

Another way you can provide support for your missionaries is to send care packages that provide that extra bit of comfort they might not provide for themselves. And don't forget to include encouraging notes and pictures from home in the package. Here are some care package ideas:

- **A comfort-food basket.** Treat your servant with nonperishable items such as hot cocoa packets, soup mixes, his or her favorite type of cookies or chips, beef jerky, biscuit mixes with jams, any item from the person's home region, and so on.

- **A spa basket.** Fill it with items such as bubble bath, an eye mask, a face scrub, hand cream, a loofah sponge, nail polish, and a bottle of Perrier.

- **A media basket.** For those who will be missing their daily doses of CNN and pop culture, include newspapers, books, entertainment magazines, tapes of recordings of their favorite shows, a bag of popcorn, and some cans or bottles of their favorite soft drink (pad your box well if you do this last one).

Keep your doings classified from your missionary. It could turn out to be a welcome surprise at just the right time.

Idea 3   Open-Door Policy

When missionary families come home on furlough, they often have a common struggle: Where are we going to live for six months, and how are we going to get around? These families sell their houses and get rid of all their possessions in their homeland and venture off to another country to serve the Lord. However, they still return home to see friends and families every couple of years—and, of course, to raise awareness and financing for their missions work.

An individual missionary can crash with a friend or family member in a spare room for the time. But for families with children, this can be a bigger challenge.

If there are families with a rental property, basement apartment, pool house, or even a second home, opening it up to the missionary family would be an incredibly generous way to meet their housing needs. Start asking the congregation months before a missionary family is scheduled to return. If the owner is in need of cash to cover costs on the property during that time, take a special collection, and ask members of your congregation to commit to regular giving for this set period of time.

Also, if there are families in your congregation with an extra car, allowing the missionary family to borrow it would be a great way to bless and show the family that your church wants to take care of their needs. Or if a family is considering buying a new car, perhaps they'd be willing to wait a few months before getting rid of the old one so it could be used by the missionaries.

Idea 4   Growing International Friendships

Missionary kids grow up with some pretty amazing experiences. Family vacations might include traveling to places like Cairo and Singapore, and while other students have pet dogs and cats, they carry slingshots to scare off pesky baboons or take public transportation through St. Petersburg, Russia, to get to school. They can speak three languages—one that's not even written down yet—and have passports filled with stamps from all over three continents. Sounds pretty exotic, right?

It might be exotic some days, but it's an experience that is hard to relate to and communicate when kids come home from assignment on furlough, or permanently. Other students their age might be insanely jealous of the world travels and international experience. But often, missionary kids wish that they'd had the chance to go to summer camp, attend a public school in their native language, be at the youth group pizza party—and in general, wish they were around for more than a couple months every few years or so. For junior and senior high students especially, relationships can make or break any experience.

In order to help students in missionary families feel more welcome and part of the group while they are home, have your students build relationships while they're abroad. Swap e-mail addresses. Match up students based on age and gender (and personal interest, if possible), and encourage them to start talking regularly. Serving this way, in such a personal manner, will foster life-changing relationships for everyone involved.

Idea 5   Feet to Feet

Shoes—we all have them. We all use them. We buy new ones because they're trendy. We toss old ones because we just don't like them anymore.

In many countries around the world, shoes are not always a given, and in fact can be quite valuable. What we consider old and worn out, they consider brand-new and a privilege.

Work with missionaries at your church. Figure out when and where short- and long-term missionaries are headed. A few months before the trip, start collecting shoes. Ask students to approach the school and make it a school project. Many schools have fundraisers and other volunteer work, and many high schoolers have worn-out shoes that are still wearable.

As your students are collecting these shoes, encourage them to share with their friends that they are doing this to spread God's love around the world by meeting the basic needs of people who can't afford the same luxuries they enjoy.

After the shoes are collected, plan a Saturday where they can be sorted, cleaned, and packed. Toss the shoes that are too worn out to share, and clean up the ones that still have life in them. You can pack them in army surplus bags. Then, when missionaries head overseas, they can take one of the bags as their second piece of luggage. The bags can be donated as well, or they can be folded up and brought back.

You could even use the shoes as the basis *for* a mission trip. Plan on partnering with a missionary from your church and ask him or her how a group could serve for a week, for two weeks, or for an extended short-term mission trip. Use taking the shoes as an excuse to go, but then take the idea a step further by bringing the people who collect the shoes into the world of a missionary. It will reach out to the missionary and give him or her a valuable connection to his or her home congregation. And as cross-cultural experiences often do, it will greatly impact the lives of those who go on the trip by opening up their eyes to how God is working to meet peoples' needs in another part of the world.

Idea 6 Traveling Mercies

Flying a family internationally costs thousands of dollars, especially for some missionaries living in remote parts of the world where airfare is even pricier. Also, once they are in the country, they often travel around the country to visit supporters and family. This gets expensive quickly and costs even more for families.

Instead of simply asking for cash for missionaries from your church to return from their assignment for furlough and to travel around the country once they are here, ask your congregation if they are interested in donating frequent-flier miles. This might be of particular interest to business travelers who collect thousands of miles a year.

You might also ask members of your congregation if they have any nights earned at hotel chains. There are probably more than a few nights when missionary families will be in need of a place to stay. Many of these are redeemable internationally.

Also, consider offering frequent-flier travel for times besides furlough. Missionaries may not have the time or be able to raise support for unexpected and special-occasion trips such as college visits for high school students, weddings, and funerals. It could even help provide missionaries a badly needed vacation!

Idea 7   "Taste of Missions" Festival

Most big cities have a "Taste of [city]" summer festival where local restaurants set up booths, and participants then sample foods from the city's best eateries. Transform this idea into a fun, family-oriented missions celebration for your church. Invite volunteers to "adopt" a specific region of the world, learn about that region's culture, read about the spiritual "climate" there, learn what missionaries in that region are doing, and select and prepare a food item from that region.

For your "Taste of Missions" festival, volunteers will set up tables and distribute tastes of their food items. (If necessary, charge a per-person fee to cover the cost of food.) Let people roam around and sample food from different countries. As people visit your booth, make a point of teaching them something about the region represented there.

As your event winds down, gather participants back together. Ask them to form subgroups of three or four, and have them discuss the following:

- Which food was your favorite? Why?

- What was something new you learned today? What areas or needs stood out to you?

- How can our church do more to help people around the world learn about Jesus?

Idea 8   Adopt a Country

Even those who never are called to leave this country can make a powerful difference in another nation. Adopt a country or a people group somewhere in the world. Learn about it and pray for everything the people do there. Contact and partner with a specific missionary or church from the region, and ask about how you can encourage and serve them. Then do it!

But don't limit yourself to prayer. Learn the culture—maybe even the language—of the country you're supporting in prayer. It's easy to keep up to date with developments in a given country via the Internet. Find out what is happening, and read it through the perspective of those serving in that area, discerning spiritual needs and praying knowledgeably about that country.

Your church or group could even invest in a shortwave radio in order to listen to broadcasts from almost any country in the world. Most have English broadcasts. Bear in mind that many of these broadcasts are sponsored by the governments of those countries, so use discernment.

God can answer our prayers for both our missionaries and the countries they serve in and can even open the way for the gospel where that way might currently be closed. Your prayers could literally change a country.

Idea 9   Do a Workcamp

Looking for something a little more hands-on to get your church— and especially your youth—more missions-minded? Check out Group Workcamps® at www.groupworkcamps.com, where there are dozens of week-long summer projects ranging from home repair to community service and outreach to international service and outreach trips.

Each year, youth groups prove to us that nothing ignites spiritual growth like putting faith into action. The results are amazing as children, youth, and adults alike get away from their homes and travel to a community with a desire to serve God. As students serve people in Christ's name (and with a little guidance and nurturing), they grow in faith and character—and have loads of fun at the same time!

Choose where you want to go together, then put *your* faith into action. You'll spend amazing times with God and with teenagers from churches around the country.

Idea 10   Prayer Buddies

Ask the kids in your church to be prayer buddies with missionary kids overseas. Talk first with your children's parents and ask their permission, then get in contact with missionaries who have younger children and do the same. Try as best you can to link children of similar ages, then remind your students to pray frequently for these children, as well as write them notes and even send small gifts once in a while.

If you do this together as a group, discuss these questions with your kids after a writing or gift-making project:

- How does exchanging letters and prayers with your prayer buddy change the way you see others? God? yourself?

- When we do outreach to serve or care for others, what do you think *we* get out of it?

- What are some other ways we can serve God by serving other children in our own neighborhoods?

Idea 11 Overnight Fast

One of the most frequently mentioned spiritual disciplines in the Bible—fasting—is one of the least practiced today. Scripture records that people fasted for a variety of specific reasons: to repent and ask forgiveness, to guide them in making difficult decisions, to ask God's favor, or even to prepare for battle. It can also be used as an opportunity to open your church's eyes to the poverty and suffering elsewhere in the world, and even in this small way make it a lot more real to them.

Introduce your church or group to this time-honored discipline by holding your own 24-hour fast. Pledge to fast from Saturday dinner to Sunday dinner. Instead of eating when you normally would, spend time in prayer and looking up Scripture passages about fasting, such as Deuteronomy 8:2-5; Esther 4:16; Daniel 9:1-3; Joel 2:12-14; or Matthew 4:1-2; 6:16-18.

On Sunday evening, break your collective fast by eating a simple meal together. Donate the money your church or group would have spent on meals to an organization that works to eradicate hunger, such as World Vision, Compassion International, or Bread for the World. Talk about what you've learned and the ways you feel closer to God as the result of your collective fast.

Idea 12 Experience Another Faith

Many Americans have not seen the worship of other cultures firsthand. It is not easy to share our faith with others—or to fully appreciate what our missionaries do every day—if we do not first understand why others worship the way they do. Churches can pray that they will understand the minds of these people and gain new insight into where missionaries work and the different kinds of issues they deal with.

Arrange a group visit to a local Hindu or Buddhist temple, Islamic mosque, Jewish synagogue, or other place of religious worship. This visit should be arranged beforehand. Listen, watch, and learn as you step inside another world.

Get involved. Speak to the religious leader(s) that you meet. Ask about their place and pattern of worship, the meaning of the religious symbols used, types of clothing and food, main beliefs, style of worship, and type of "church" administration. Also ask these religious leaders what they think of Christians, what their main concerns are about how Christians conduct themselves, and what Christians can do to have better relations with them.

Most non-Christian religions are open to having visitors and will offer generous hospitality when you show up. Some are missionary faiths; others are not. Some religions, like Islam, work hard to make converts, and some mosques even have their own outreach directors.

Share your experience with your friends at your church group. In small groups of three or four, discuss the following questions:

- What affected you the most about what you saw?

- What similarities or contradictions did you notice between their faith and yours?

- What did you learn about sharing Jesus with this particular religious group? What steps will you take to connect with these people in the future?

Idea 13   "Prepare for Landing" Party

Many people realize how difficult it can be to pack up and move to another region of the world as a missionary. Few people realize that packing up and moving back home is often even more difficult. The re-entry process for missionaries can be a time of disillusionment, depression, and stress as they leave behind a big part of their lives. Missionaries are often sent off amid hoopla but often come home unnoticed. You can be a tremendous support and make the homecoming a soft landing by organizing a "Prepare for Landing" party.

Communicate with the missionary and find out his or her specific needs. Some common ones are a car, a place to stay, a job, kitchen and pantry supplies, furniture, or a computer.

Announce the homecoming at your church a month or two in advance, and keep the announcements coming every week or two. Get your congregation eager to celebrate! Ask church members to provide for the returning missionary's needs, leaving the list of needs some place where they can sign up.

If the missionary is serving a church or organization abroad, contact that organization for pictures, letters, and stories about the person's service. If you get enough pictures, create a scrapbook or a slide show set to music to show at the party. To honor the missionary at the party, make sure to read the stories or letters.

Have the party very soon after the missionary's return—within a week or two. And make it a celebration! Share how that person's work has affected others. Here are some other ideas:

- Provide a welcome-home care package that includes small items the person will need, such as cleaning supplies, toilet paper, and pantry items. This package could also contain items native to his or her home. (Perhaps he or she has been missing Cheetos desperately!)

- Serve food and play music of the region from which he or she is returning.

- Allow the missionary time to share stories with the whole group.

And *most importantly,* don't let the support and encouragement stop there. *Continue* to help with the logistics of moving to a new country, and provide emotional and spiritual support for the challenges the missionary will continue to face as he or she re-enters society here.

Help your group experience outreach like never before...natural, everyday, overflowing.
Read this excerpt from *Outflow* -- the book that inspires, empowers, and equips people to reach out with God's love.

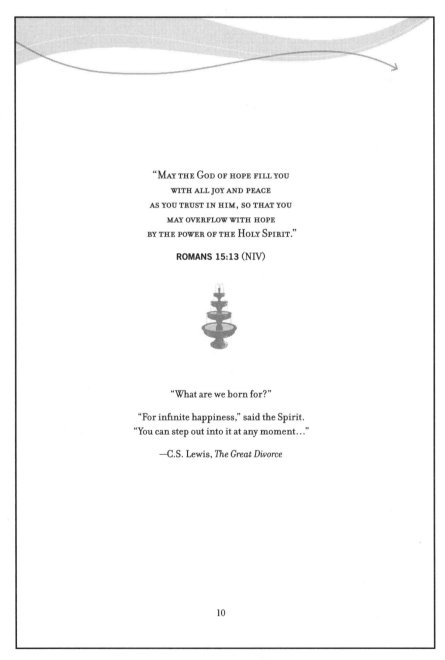

"MAY THE GOD OF HOPE FILL YOU
WITH ALL JOY AND PEACE
AS YOU TRUST IN HIM, SO THAT YOU
MAY OVERFLOW WITH HOPE
BY THE POWER OF THE HOLY SPIRIT."

ROMANS 15:13 (NIV)

"What are we born for?"

"For infinite happiness," said the Spirit.
"You can step out into it at any moment…"

—C.S. Lewis, *The Great Divorce*

10

Available from Group Publishing

READING 1

experiencing outflow

Splash...A tiny drop of rain fell from heaven as Theresa's dented Toyota idled roughly in the Taco Bell drive-through. A single mom, she depended on a government welfare check to feed her 8-year-old son. It was 10 days till the next check would arrive and she was already broke. Here's how she described what happened:

> After looking under the sofa cushions, all the car seats, and through the glove box, we came up with a grand total of...$4.58! It had been a hard week and my thinking was, "Hey, any way you look at it we aren't going to have enough money to make it through to the next check. So let's go out with style." So we headed for Taco Bell.
>
> As we got to the drive thru window to pay, I was never so shocked in all of my life. The guy standing in the window had a big grin on his face and said, "This is your lucky day—the people in front of you paid for your entire meal. They said to give you this card."
>
> The card read, "We hope this *small act of service* shows you God's love in a practical way," but I've got to tell you something, for me and my 8-year-old son, Donny, this was no *small* act of love. It was *huge*. We were in exactly the right place at exactly the right time to receive this touch from God when we needed it most!

The next day, Theresa and Donny came to church for the very first time. That tiny drop of generosity they'd experienced in God's name made them hopeful that perhaps God really did care about them and what they were going through.

11

Available from Group Publishing

12   _OUTFLOW_

A Promise From God

Maybe, like Theresa, you've wondered about God. Does God exist? Does he really care about me? Are God and religion even relevant anymore? My life is filled with technology, busyness, and modern problems—what, honestly, does an old-fashioned God have to do with my life?

Or maybe you already know God. Maybe you're asking different questions…questions like: How can I have a deeper relationship with God? How can I have a more authentic faith—one that's reflected in every part of my life? How can I trust God for my health, finances, and future? How can I share my hope in God with the people around me?

It doesn't matter where we are in our faith—on which part of the belief spectrum we're standing—we all have questions. We have deeply rooted and deeply critical questions. Questions whose answers will ultimately define the way we live.

The _Outflow_ book is dedicated to exploring some of these difficult questions and God's biblical promises. Promises that answer our questions. Promises whose essential messages boil down to this:

Your life is meant to overflow with unimaginable joy and power.

As you read the sentence above, you might have been thinking, "No way! Maybe that's possible for extraordinarily holy people like Mother Teresa or Billy Graham, but not for everyday people like me!" And if these promises came from anywhere south of heaven, you would be right. They would seem completely ridiculous. But the fact is they come directly from the mouth of the Lord, and they permeate the very fabric of both the Old and New Testaments:

> "The Lord will guide you always; he will satisfy your needs in a sun-scorched land and will strengthen your frame. You will be like a well-watered garden, like a spring whose waters never fail" (ISAIAH 58:11, NIV).

> "Everyone who drinks this water will be thirsty again, but whoever drinks the water I give him will never thirst. Indeed, the water I give

him will become in him a spring of water welling up to eternal life" (JOHN 4:13-14, NIV).

If that doesn't add a little credibility, our advice is to give *Outflow* a try for the next few weeks and, as the Bible says, "Taste and see that the Lord is good" (PSALM 34:8).

Here's a story of how our friend Lynne first tasted the joy of this over-flowing life we're talking about:

66

I met Gail many years ago at our husbands' office Christmas party. After doing the small-talk thing, we realized we were both stay-at-home moms with young children. I tried hard not to cringe visibly as Gail wearily described her life to me. She'd just moved to town recently and was housebound most of the time taking care of her three children—*all of them less than 3 years old!*

I was stressed-out just taking care of my 4-year-old. I couldn't even imagine how hard it would be to care for *three* little ones, and without the help and support of local friends or family. I was getting worn out just thinking about it.

Which might explain why I stopped thinking about it, because, to be honest, I'd completely forgotten about Gail and her struggles until a few days later.

At that point I'd just started getting serious about Jesus in my life so I was new at the whole prayer thing. But after I'd asked God to bless me and my family and a few of my friends, Gail came back to mind. So I asked God to please send her someone to give her a day off from her parenting duties. When I was finished, I was feeling pretty good about what a sensitive Christian I'd become. But God wasn't quite done yet. As I stood up and went about my business, I got the sense that God wanted me to be part of his answer to my prayer for Gail.

I needed a little prompting, but after thinking about it for a bit, I got her number and gave her a call. "Gail," I said, "You may not remember me, but we met at the Christmas party last week. Yes, I enjoyed meeting you, too. Today I'm calling because I'm convinced your heavenly Father loves you so much he wants to give you a full day off."

As you might imagine, Gail wasn't exactly sure how to respond to that. After her silence had stretched for several long seconds, I jumped in.

"I'm serious. You pick a day and I'll come over and take care of your kids from 9:00 in the morning until you're ready to come home that evening. You can go anywhere you want and do whatever you want." After another pause, Gail said it was nice of me to offer and she would think about it.

Sensing that she wasn't quite sure, I pressed on. "Just pick a day and I'll come over. And if you don't pick a day, I'm going to show up anyway." And, in the end, that's how it happened. I showed up at her house one morning. After she decided I wasn't crazy or a criminal, she gave in and agreed to let me watch her kids. That's when I told her I'd reserved a hotel room in her name if she wanted to have a nice place to take a nap—and that I wouldn't be upset if she didn't use it.

Gail left the house and didn't return again until 9:30 that evening. When she walked in the kids were all tucked in bed, her husband was watching TV, and I had dinner waiting for her. A smile on her face, Gail asked, "Why did you say you were doing this?"

Once again, I said simply, "Because your heavenly Father wants you to know he loves you!"

Something in Gail changed that day. The long hours away from her house and children caused her to recognize that she'd been suffocating emotionally, all the while never asking her husband or anyone else for help. After that day she finally had the courage to ask. And when she did ask, Gail was amazed at how willing he and others were to help lighten her load.

I thought all this was a great answer to my prayer, but God wasn't done yet. There was something even more exciting to come. A couple of weeks later, Gail called me up on the phone. "Tell me again, why did you decide to help me?" she asked.

Available from Group Publishing

And for the third time, I repeated, "Because your heavenly Father wants you to know he loves you!"

I could hear her quietly crying in the background for several seconds before she whispered, "I want to know him."

Gail talked to Jesus for the first time that day. She recognized she needed a savior and began a friendship with him.

Again you might think this would be a good end to the story, but no. A few months after that phone call, Gail began a ministry in her church—one specifically designed to give practical help to mothers of young children!

It's a life overflowing. A life that looks a lot like what Jesus describes:

"Whoever believes in me…streams of living water will flow from within him" (JOHN 7:38, NIV).

And, in this case, it all began with Lynne believing in God enough to release his love and let it overflow from her life to Gail's. Through Lynne's caring actions and simple words, God poured living water into the thirsty places of Gail's life until she began believing…and overflowing, too.

It's so refreshing, so *incredible* to feel God's love cascading into you and through you to others. It's like Lynne says, "I don't know how to describe it, other than to say I experienced God's *intense pleasure* at what we'd accomplished together that day and all that flowed out of it. "This," she declares, "is what I was made for. I want more!"

Jars of Clay

If you're still thinking you're unworthy or inadequate or that you don't know enough, perhaps you've never heard what the Bible says about "everyday people." Hard as it may be to believe, God fills our flawed and imperfect lives with his perfect Holy Spirit. This is best described in 2 Corinthians 4:7: "But we have this treasure in jars of clay to show that this all-surpassing power is from God and not from us" (NIV).

Available from Group Publishing

Did you get that? God has put *his treasure* in us—even though we are like jars of clay, inadequate and unworthy of holding such a precious thing. But God has given us this *all-surpassing power* (do you believe that God has given you that kind of power?) so that he might be glorified through us.

It's humbling, but as Lynne so aptly pointed out, *it's what we're made for.* God created us for this kind of life—this overflowing, abundant, rich life. God made each of us a vessel—a unique jar of clay—to be filled and overflowing with his love, grace, joy, and power.

It's beautiful. It's true. And it's what the rest of this book is all about.

A Lifestyle, Not a Program

Our goal in writing this book is not to simply give you one more interesting program or Bible study to inspire and entertain you. No, we want to help you discover and tap into a refreshing *new kind of life*—one in which you are constantly drinking in the fresh, invigorating water of heaven's goodness and pouring it out into the lives of everyone around you.

And along the way, you'll notice some changes. Your relationship with God will start to feel different...more natural, more fluid. And as your friendship with God changes and grows, we believe you'll also notice your relationships at home, work, in your neighborhood, and even at church becoming fresher—more powerful.

Instead of adding another self-help book to your shelves, we wanted to put a *practical field guide* into your hands. *Outflow* is a guide to personally connecting with God and loving everyone you meet into a friendship with Christ—all in refreshingly natural ways. Check it out...

First, *Outflow* is a *practical field guide*, which means it's about actually *doing* things rather than just talking about theories or telling inspiring stories. Sure, we'll do a little of that, too; but the main event is always about translating good thinking into helpful actions. And it's a field guide, which means *Outflow* should be used *out in the field*. It's filled with sensible, useful advice to help you get around better in the environment where you're living and working.

To many reading this book, *connecting with* God probably still sounds a little theoretical, while to others it's a fact of your everyday existence. No matter where you are in your faith and relationship with God, this is a book that will help you move forward. It's about relating with Jesus in some of the same ways you do with your best friends. It's about feeling his love more truly and deeply than ever—and loving Jesus in the ways that mean the most to him. It's also about sharing the riches of this wonderful relationship by loving everybody around you closer and closer to him.

When we say *loving everybody toward Christ*, we're talking about relating to people in ways that say, "You're precious to God, and he wants you to know it." We're not just talking about religious words, but thoughtful actions and focused sharing—the kind that really helps people to *see* and *feel* God's love. And when we say *everybody*, we're talking about you, your family, your husband or wife, your boyfriend or girlfriend, your sports buddies or shopping companions. We're talking about the folks you work with, go to school with, barbecue with, or sit with to watch your child's soccer game. We're also talking about your waiters, barbers, professors, garbage collectors, gardeners, receptionists, tax accountants, people you're barely acquainted with, and total absolute strangers. No one gets left out.

Finally, when we say that you can do all of this in *refreshingly natural ways*, well, that's just what we mean. It's not about dutifully struggling your way through scripted agendas or mumbling impersonal religious slogans. It's not about guilt or doing it because you're a Christian and you feel like you should. Instead, it's about truly understanding your relationship with God. It's about having an authentic friendship with God and living free of guilt and worry—living with *confidence* and *power* in God's Spirit. Once you've got that, your desire for service and outreach will flow naturally *from* your relationship with God. You'll find yourself *really* caring for everyone around you—for their present needs and their eternal ones. You'll genuinely want to connect with the essential things that make them tick. And in doing so, you'll discover a wonderful richness in your friendships and a depth of connection you probably never dreamed possible.

It sounds great, right? If not a little…idealistic. Well, we'll understand if you're still a bit skeptical at this point. After all, we've only told you about *Outflow* and how it works…you haven't experienced it for yourself yet. But just wait, once you've experienced the blessings of living an outward-focused, overflowing life you'll never be the same—and neither will the people around you!

So come on…take the plunge. We think you'll find the water to be just right.

Outflow: Outward-Focused Living in a Self-Focused World
Get a copy for yourself, your small group, your church.

Turn this page to learn more about *Outflow*.

Available from Group Publishing

OUTFLOW

everyday outreach for everyday people

Redefining how outreach is done...
creative, natural, and effective.

PASTOR KIT
- *Outflow* Book – 256 pages
- Message Guide Book – 144 pages
- Sermon Clips DVD
- Sermon Slides/Publicity CD-ROM
- Worship Leader's DVD

978-0-7644-3399-3 **$39.99**

SMALL GROUP LEADER KIT
- *Outflow* Book – 256 pages
- Small Group DVD
- *Outflow* Music DVD

978-0-7644-3400-6 **$24.99**

YOUTH LEADER KIT
- *Outflow* Youth Journal – 96 pages
  *(Also offered separately for $4.99
  ISBN 978-0-7644-3403-7)*
- Youth Leader Guide – 80 pages
- Youth DVD

978-0-7644-3401-3 **$24.99**

CHILDREN'S LEADER KIT
- Children's Leader Guide – 80 pages
- Children's CD
- Throw and Tell Ball: Attention Grabber

978-0-7644-3402-0 **$24.99**

FREEBIES INCLUDE:
- All publicity materials
- 52 weeks of outreach tips
- Access to an online outreach message board

Group

Incredible things will happen™

www.group.com/outflow   1-800-447-1070

Available from Group Publishing